Building a winning business strategy

Steven Farmer

Copyright © 2018 Steven Farmer
All rights reserved.

ISBN:-10: 1985185938
ISBN-13: 978-1985185937

DEDICATION

This book is dedicated to my loving and supportive wife Clare, my son Thomas, my two dogs Bailey and Tiggy and my three miniature mediteranean donkeys, Dudley, Blossom and Josie; without whom life would be very dull.

CONTENTS

Table of Contents

Acknowlegements v
1 The dark art of strategy 1
2 Start at the beginning 6
3 The discovery phase toolkit 10
4 Competitive Strategies 36
5 The build phase 40
6 Put your employees first 48
7 The sales strategy 56
8 Scenario Planning 77
9 Selling the vision 87
10 Culture 95
11 Execution 103
12 The Balanced Scorecard 121
13 Holding each other to account 131
14 Bringing it all together 133

Acknowlegements

I would like to thank all who I have worked with over the years for the lessons and examples that our triumphs and failures have taught us. Special thanks go to Alison Bond and Clare Farmer for proofing my manuscript and giving encouraging feedback and also to Jack Night who's illustrations have helped bring my scribbled illustrations to reality.

1 The dark art of strategy

"Like strategy, innovation is a cool word. Put strategy and innovation in a single phrase and a strategy tourist starts drooling." Anon.

I have a career spanning over 30 years in the construction, rail and engineering industries and during that time I have made my way from site based apprentice up the proverbial corporate ladder. When you get half way up the ladder and start making the lofty ascents into senior management, increasingly people talk about being a strategic thinker as well as being able to think outside of the box and see the bigger picture. I have heard peers passing judgement on their colleagues saying things like "they are just not strategic enough" or they are "not operating at a high enough level". When looking for a career move you may see requirements relating to having strategic vision and being able to deliver the strategy which always seems to either be based on delivering double digit growth or steering the company towards their chosen number one position in whatever industry they are operating in.

At the age of 26 I did not really know what I wanted out of my life but I was ambitious and keen to keep moving forwards so I jumped at the chance of professional development sponsorship and enrolled on what would turn out to be a seven year journey through academia in business and management to get my MBA. As I was researching for my studies I developed a love for reading which had eluded me all the way through my years in full time formal education. I have since read hundreds of books on strategy, sales, negotiating skills, influence, persuasion, engagement and performance management as well as having played out what I have learned in the business world as an MD and CEO to varying degrees of success. The use of the term varying degrees of success may seem a little strange as I'm obviously trying to build my credibility with you as the reader but anyone who has been in a business leadership position for any reasonable period of time would have experienced the ebbs and flows and ups and downs of things both inside and outside of your control, irrespective of where you sit in the organisation and how good or hard working and diligent you are. Having had both success and failure, I speak with experience when I say that failures are inevitable in all businesses and the best thing to do is make sure that you learn from them so you are not condemned to repeat them. Some of the greatest lessons in business come from failures so make sure you take the time to reflect on what went wrong and take the learnings from them. All the greatest learning happens on the edge of your comfort zone, so embrace failures and embrace the lessons that failure gives you. Some people think that success and failure are at opposite ends of the spectrum but failure plays a part in every successful endeavour.

When considering the title for this book I thought long and hard about whether to call it - *How not to fail at business strategy*. In terms of broad appeal for such a book the significant majority of strategies do fail, about 70% in fact. I also considered this title because people generally hate failing more than they enjoy winning but in the end I wanted to keep the title free from the word fail as despite my belief that failure is a means to an end, not everybody shares this view. It's worth noting here that there is also a saying that nothing fails like past success and simply applying the same successful strategic solution in different organisational contexts can be a shortcut to overconfident failure. Although it would seem obvious that successful strategy should be about culture, context, positioning and that invariably none of these are ever the same, it's an important learning that rather than having a step by step strategic process and a one size fits all approach, it's probably more important to think about strategy as a toolbox that you build up and have at your disposal, then dependent on any given situation you can use the right strategic tool for the job. There is a logical process to follow when developing your strategy but there are a range of choices that need to be made along the way. Hopefully when choosing this book you were drawn to the prospect of winning and there is a world of difference in attitude between winning and not failing. If all your business decisions are centred around not failing, then it will be unlikley that you will be ready for and to acccept the risks associated with playing to win when the right opportunities present themselves. Using this book will give you the confidence to make the right choices whilst reducing the chances of losing. I have drawn upon my own business lessons aswell as some public high profile business sucesses and failures which we now have the benefit of 20:20 hindsight. The cautionary tale with some of these examples is that these businesses were full of very bright and hardworking people that analysed their strategic marketplace and were trying to come out on top. In business there can be no guarantees around who will win and who will loose but there are valuable lessons we can take from whats happening in the wider business world.

My motive for writing this book is a simple one, I want to share what I have learned and provide you with the tools, expertise and confidence to build your own winning business strategy without you feeling or being made to feel inferior because you never enrolled at the MBA school of black arts and strategic wizidary. This book is for the thousands of aspiring middle and senior managers who feel like their next step up the corporate ladder are being unnecessarily blocked or their performance review and development needs are couched in disappointment through not being given the right guidance, support and advice to develop their own strategic thinking. This book will also benefit the successful entrepreneurs and owner managers who are looking for the right kind of advice and clarity on how to take their businesses to the next level without the need for expensive management consultants. As well as giving practical tools and advice on the creation of a winning strategy, the book touches on some of the softer but significantly more difficult aspects of successful strategic execution and how to ensure that your companies culture does not kill your strategy before it has even been fully rolled out.

I would like to take this opportunity to thank you for buying this book and I'm looking forward to sharing your own strategic journey with you and providing everything you need to build your own winning business strategy. The book is designed to be read either from cover to cover or you can dip into the various sections and use it as a reference to guide your strategic thinking. I have included a comprehensive bibliography and references to further reading materials. After reading this book you will be fully equipped to not only build your own strategy, but you will have the confidence to hold your own in any meeting or boardroom situation where strategy is talked about. What you will find most revealing is that when you have insight and understanding of what makes a good strategy you will be better equipped to identify ill thought through or non existent strategies that are disguised in a barrage of buzz words and a wish list of nothing more than goals espoused as corporate strategy. You will also notice that invariably the people that like to talk about the strategy the most are the ones who know precious little about it. This book will present you with the right kind of positive opportunities to contribute to the strategic planning and develop your skills as a strategic practitioner to redress the balance. In the latter stages of this book I will also give you some guidance on what is fundamentally the most important part of any strategy and strangely enough it's the bit they don't teach you at business school. There are CEO's and MD's in offices up and down the country who have the most comprehensive and elaborate business strategies with market analysis, charts, competitor analysis, planned growth in revenue and operating profit forecasts that would make them the envy of any of their peers. They commission external consultants to produce the strategies that leave no MBA model or stone unturned and yet as the strategy starts to gather dust and become increasingly less relevant) apart from them periodically reaching for it to show their bosses or financial backers that they do indeed have a viable strategy), they begin to wonder what went wrong and how the promised fortunes of all the multicolored charts never actually materialized. The biggest single problem with even the very best strategies is that 70% of them fail[1] and this is not down to the quality of the strategy it's down to poor execution of the strategy. Most leaders seem to forget that the strategy is the roadmap that gets you to the starting line and gives you direction, they also forget that unless the strategy is shared and clearly articulated to the people that really matter, the strategy is doomed to failure. Rarely do strategies come crashing down like cleanly felled trees, instead they die slowly over a period of a couple of years where the managers end up blaming the leader and the leader blames the managers citing that they had produced the perfect strategy that should make sense to everyone. The problem with some leaders with MBA's in my opinion is that they produce a strategy to prove to everyone just how clever they are, when they should be focussing on producing a strategy that demonstrates how connected they are to the people and their organisation. The very best business leaders are the ones that can make the connections between the need to satisfy the shareholders and the need to give each and every one of their employees something meaningful to get out of bed for. The more traditional leaders somehow think that simply paying someone's salary is all the motivation and engagement that they will need to diligently make themselves familiar with the business strategy and follow it to the letter. The secret with strategic delivery and execution is engagement and commitment to the

---

[1] McKinsey research shows a 70% strategic failure rate

strategy and leaving the engagement of the workforce to chance in this way is the single biggest source of strategic failure in businesses today. Do not worry because help is at hand and this book is not just about building a strategy, it's about building a winning business strategy and of course to win you have to show up and take part.

Figure 1 - How to stop getting invited to strategic presentations

---

[i] Chandler, Alfred *Strategy and Structure: Chapters in the history of industrial enterprise*, Doubleday, New York, 1962.

2 Start at the beginning

Any intelligent fool can make things bigger and more complex. It takes a touch of genius – and a lot of courage – to move in the opposite direction"—Albert Einstein

Before we begin it is probably worth just taking a moment to consider what do we mean by strategy as its often an overused word which goes unquestioned and unexamined. Over the last forty years the number of books on strategy have grown from just a few in the 1960's to a whole section offering you a strategy on just about anything. We now have marketing strategies, sales strategies, IT strategies, social media strategies, employee engagement strategies, the list goes on. On close examination of many large corporate strategies they are generally nothing more than a list of corporate goals that do not offer either a roadmap on how to get the desired results or contain any insight into the market or competition. The goals are the outcomes but strategy is fundamentally about choices, sometimes these are alternate choices between competing courses of action or it may be the choice between saying yes or no to another. The worst examples of strategy are seamingly designed to deliberately confuse and will over complicate the language used without the offer of any clarification or further explanations by the author(s). Many poor but elaborate strategies offer up a cunning disguise of a company's biggest strategic issues like poor employee relations or customer service but wax lyrical about growth in market share and double digit profits. A strategy is supposed to take a medium to long term view but this should not mean that the companies problems in the foreground can be overlooked. Often people are afraid in the strategy presentations to ask for exploration of say the difference between strategy, objectives, goals and tactics through fear of being ridiculed or showing their lack of knowledge and how this may impact how they are judged by others. In truth if you ask everyone around the table to write down their understanding of the word strategy, invariably you will have as many variants as you will people.

A good place to start is with the Oxford English dictionary definition of strategy in business as "*A plan of action designed to achieve a long-term or overall aim*", which of course offers a very distinct bonus if it is in turn linked to the overall objectives of the shareholders and the stakeholders in the business. There are other equally elegant definitions of strategy offered up by strategy guru's such as Alfred Chandler, who in 1962 wrote that: "*Strategy is the determination of the basic long-term goals of an enterprise, and the adoption of courses of action and the allocation of resources necessary for carrying out these goals.*"[i]

Michael Porter in 1980 defined strategy as "*"...broad formula for how a business is going to compete, what its goals should be, and what policies will be needed to carry out those goals*" and the "*...combination of the ends (goals) for which the firm is striving and the means (policies) by which it is seeking to get there.*"[ii] As well as focusing on the strategic objectives of your own organisation it is important that you take into account and have sufficient insight of what's happening in your industry and ideally the comparative advantages between your own service offering and that of your competition. Later in this book I will provide the tools and frameworks so that you can further explore the context in which your business operates but the essential thing to get right from the beginning of the strategy formulation process is to objectively and truthfully assess the genuine strengths and weaknesses of your own offering and how these best serve your customers.

In the immortal words taken from one of Stephen Covey's seven habits of highly effective people, you need to begin with the end in mind. You should not prepare a strategy just because your business has reached a certain size and you feel like you should have one, neither should you prepare a strategy to prove you know how to put one together. If strategy is about the attainment of the basic long term goals of an enterprise this in itself can be a powerful process by which you can flush out and truly understand if the people in your senior team share the same vision for where the business is heading. Your own particular end in mind may not be a definitive destination for the business at some fixed point in the future, it may well be more of an ambition of what service or product space you would like to move towards on the understanding that further adjustments will be made as the technology, customer requirements and the market dictates over time. The point I am making here is not to let yourself off the hook with your end in mind by saying the strategic direction is constantly changing etc. The old saying that failing to plan is planning to fail also holds true with long term strategic objectives. In a rapidly changing and dynamic marketplace there is a fundamental requirement to constantly scan the strategic landscape and make the adjustments as necessary. The days of the rigid five year strategic plan are over particularly in an age when companies are born, change the world and then in some cases die all within a 5 year time horizon (MySpace, Netscape). Instead you should look at your strategic plan as being analogous to the flight plan of a commercial airliner, where effectively you are off course for 95% of the journey but you are constantly monitoring your feedback systems and making course adjustments. There are no excuses for the refrains such as "our business is so dynamic and fast moving its pointless to have a strategy as it will have changed by the time the ink is dry". I have also heard leaders say that their strategy is to be number 1 in the market place with little or no substance to back up such statements. All strategic intents should be questioned and pressure tested in the context of the organisation and its ability to commit resources, build on its competitive advantages and to exploit the weaknesses of the competition. Without understanding where you are now, what cards you hold and what you will do to strengthen your hand relative to the competition, the use of empty statements and platitudes is either a none strategy or even worse a bad strategy. In some cases a bad strategy can actually speed up the demise of an organisation that only becomes apparent when the administrators have been called in. The history books are littered with failed companies that had seemingly fumbled away a strong strategic position by failing to recognize that its market place was shifting out from underneath it. The DVD rental store Blockbuster famously passed over an opportunity to buy Netflix thinking incorrectly that its core activity was in the DVD home rental business and not more accurately as a payment on demand or subscription home entertainment business. At the time of writing Blockbusters are no more and the Netflix market capitalisation is larger than Disney making it the worlds largest entertatinment business. In the USA Sam Walton grew Walmart by opening stores that went against the K-Mart conventional wisdom of only opening stores with a local customer base of greater than 100,000 local residents. K-Mart completely misunderstood it's competition and subsequently failed to realise until it was way too late that Walmart's use of technology and what we now call supply chain management significantly lowered its cost base to bring down the point at which stores became viable to serve local communities. As mentioned earlier, nothing fails like past successes and businesses that have grown rapidly in size based on strategic beliefs and dogma need to be wary of what can become a kind of cognitive blindness to what is going on in the marketplace around them.

This chapter is called start at the beginning and it's ok to begin with the end in mind so you get everyone on the same page as to what the destination looks like. The problem that is often avoided in most business strategies is that they are so busy looking to the future that they either forget or deliberately ignore current business challenges in their marketplace relating to competition, innovation, changing customer requirements, talent and skills retention. Invariably there are always short term thorny issues that need to be faced into that should be the ultimate starting point for any business strategy.

Figure 2 Elephant blindness in 1982 leads to K-Mart Collapse in 2002

3 The discovery phase toolkit

"If all you have is a hammer, everything looks like a nail"
Bernard Baruch

Having guarded against the over complication of strategy, this next section is full of simple but powerful concepts to help you achieve clarity on the strategic issues facing your own business. They say a picture speaks a thousand words so anything that can simplify the context, the issues and the message should be encouraged. In much the same way as you should guard against only using a single tool I would also counsel against using them all. I'm in danger of mixing my metaphors here but if you imagine a golfer with a full set of golf clubs, they will choose the appropriate club for each shot based on distance, lie of the ball etc derived from their own judgement of the situation. They may complete a full 18 hole round of golf having only used half of their golf clubs but on the same course a week later they may need them all. My toolkit on strategy formulation is all about keeping things simple and the reason I deliberately do this is that ultimately you need to have your audience in mind. I will come onto the execution of the strategy in later chapters but at some point you and your senior will need to sell to the rest of your organisation how you have formulated the strategy and what has been considered, addressed and discarded along the way. With the 70% failure rate of strategies at the execution stage, keeping your messages clear will help in the transference of enthusiasm and significantly aid adoption and engagement for the strategy on launch day and beyond. The toolkit is by no means exhaustive but I have built and delivered a number of strategies and periodically I find myself on the receiving end of a new concept worthy of the collection. I have deliberately included lots of tools for the discovery phase of the strategic process as this is by far the most important. Imagine you arrive at work one morning and an announcement is made that a new five year strategic process is going to be launched, this comes as a surprise as this comes just three years into the previous but by now failing five year strategy. The CEO has taken decisive action stating that we all need to redouble our efforts to make up the perceived lost ground as the previous strategy is not quite delivering what the business expected. The CEO then sets a new stretch target and invariably this will be limited to a sales and Earnings Before Interest Tax Depreciation and Amortization (EBITDA) figure as she pulls together a team for the strategic refresh. In short the EBITDA is an accounting term relating to the cash profitability of the business. One of the team dusts off the three year old elaborately bound strategy that has not been opened for at least two years and the team all agree that some really good work was done on alnalysing the idustry competitiveness and this is still equally relevant so they skip over this crucial element of the strategic build to get on with the more interesting and self-affirming aspects of playing with Excel spreadsheets and extrapolating the sales and profit forecast graphs to hit the CEO's desired new numbers. You may feel that this kind of scenario is over exaggerated but I have been in businesses where this is pretty close to the truth. The initial discovery phase is by far the most important and just like in the medical field, prescription before diagnosis is malpractice. I would urge you to take as much time as is necessary on the discovery phase because when failed businesses get picked over in the press generally you will find the reasons for the failure either absent or included but generally ignored from the actual effective implementation of the strategy. In businesses where the CEO has said the new five year target is £100M sales, implicitly the whole strategy team sets to work on identifying the truths that will make this possible and generally ignoring the fundamental truths that would need to be faced into to make the business a success. A key message here is take your time on the discovery phase as all successful businesses are built on a thorough understanding of reality. You cannot expect to shoot for the stars if you cannot even achieve a stable orbit.

"When describing how he would use one hour to solve a problem, Albert Einstein said that he would first spend 55 minutes precisely clarifying the question. Once the problem was crystal clear, he would only need five minutes to come up with an answer."

(S.W.O.T) Strengths, Weaknesses, Opportunities and Threats

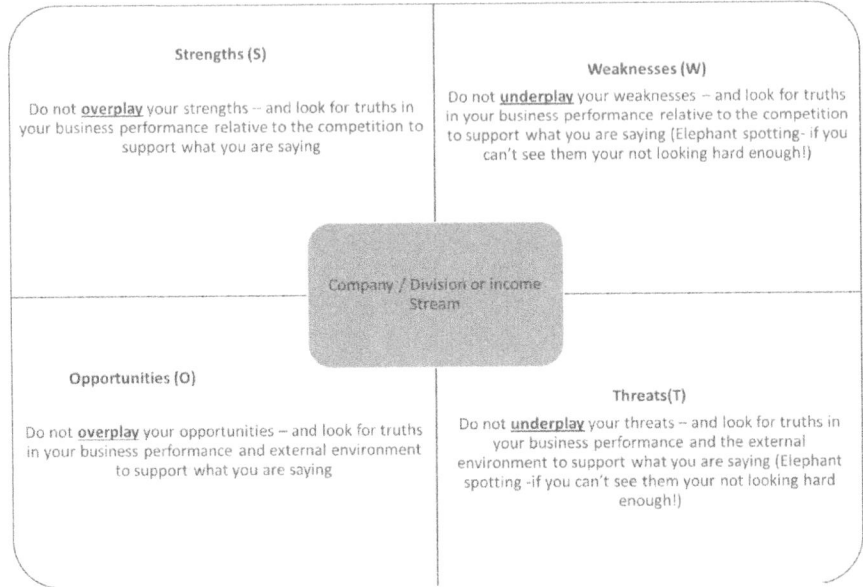

Figure 3 S.W.O.T Analysis - simple but skip past this at your peril!

Make sure you take the appropriate amount of time to really dig deep and truly understand the issues. When companies complete the Strengths, Weaknesses, Opportunities and Threats (S.W.O.T) analysis they tend to grossly under estimate the threats and weaknesses and conversely over estimate their strengths and opportunities. At the time of writing this chapter yet another large multi-national organisation has gone into administration and been dragged before a UK parliamentary commission to explain what went wrong. The chairman accepted full responsibility blaming a family of elephants called Brexit, bad contracts and overseas markets. I do not know which is the worst of the two evils, either not recognising and understanding the warning signs or fully recognising the warning signs and not having the courage or conviction as a senior team to take the necessary actions and do something about it.

PESTEL ANALYSIS

This is a little like the S.W.O.T analysis and is another planning method to be used in the discovery phase. Where S.W.O.T analysis is situational and relates to the your particular product or service offerring, the PESTEL analysis is more about what is going on in the macro or country level environment that may impact the market environment, that you, your customers and your competition operate in.

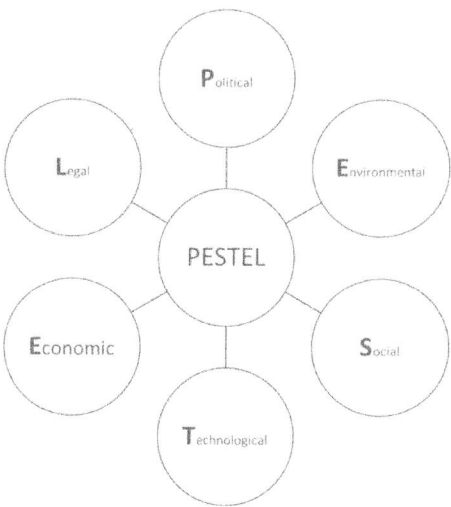

Figure 4 PESTEL analysis

Political – could there be any government legislation that effects either the economy as a whole or your chosen marketplace. For examplke macro economic impacts of a general election, the UK Brexit vote or the smoking ban for the tobacco industry are all recent political impacts on the marketplace in the UK.

Economic - Factors include – economic growth, interest rates, exchange rates, inflation, disposable income of consumers and businesses and so on. This will level the playing field in your country of operation as you and your in country competition will be dealing with the same issues. If you are competing internationally this can give you a comparative advantage or disadvatage dependant on foreign exchange rates and the international economic conditions. At the micro economic level this is more about how consumers spend their money and in a tight economic situation this can significantly impact your market if your are selling business to consumer (B2C), particulary if your product or service is classed as a luxury item. One of my favourite examples of the economies impact on the business to consumer market is the sale of popcorn at cinemas. It seems that in bad times and good the country like to visit the cinema but in tough economic times, the sale of popcorn suffers dramatically. I remember reading a BBC article in 2009 about the increased sales of popcorn at the cinema being one of the early measurements of green shoots for economic recovery. The national Cinema chains will see an upturn in popcorn sales upto 6 weeks before other conventional economic indictors start to move in the right direction.

Social - these factors include – population growth, age distribution, health consciousness, career attitudes and so on. How people buy products and services and how they want to be marketed and communicated to is linked to changes in the social environment. Your social consideration should also adress not only your customers but your own workforce. You will not be able to adequately address the social needs of your customers without first addressing the needs of your workforce. By 2020 millennials will form 50% of the global workforce[2] and they will expect greater flexibility and work life integration that will move away from the traditional concept of 9 to 5 working and work life balance. The edges between work and familiy life will continue to blur which will create a new competitive landscape for the acquisition and retention of talent. Your customers will become increasingly conscious about how you operate in the local and wider community including what your values and sustainability vision are.

---

[2] Pwc report

Technological – this effects the production, distribution and marketing of products and is an ever changing landscape. The introduction of 5G networks and the increasing amounts of connections to the Internet Of Things (IoT) will be a massive disrupter for many traditional business models as we enter the 2020's. Very few industries will escape the impact of increased automation and robotics, Artificial Intelligence (AI) and new ways of using technology which will impact every part of our lives. The response to the technological challenge can be every bit as dangerous as doing nothing at all. If you place big company bets on an emerging technology that subsequently falls by the wayside this can mean the end of your business, but if you are too cautious you could get left behind and lose a critical amout of market share. Even the technological guru's have been known to get things wrong when considering the future, Bill Gates once said that the internet was a novelty that would make way for something much better[3]. In January 2007 when Apple launched the first iPhone, the leadership team at Blackberry with 50% of the handset market were not the slightest bit concerned and they ridiculed the Apple iPhone for lack of a physical button keypad and poor battery life.

Environmental - Over the last 15 – 20 years both individual consumers and businesses have become more sustainably conscious which has driven significant changes across a number of markets. The automotive industry used to compete on 0-60mph times and now they compete on the lowest $Co2$ emissions. Consumers want products that are environmentally friendly with biodegradable packaging. Increasingly marketing departments are taking the sustainability of the product or service as the lead for the battle for market share. The UK government has made a commitment to reduce carbon emmissions by 57% compared to 1990 levels by 2050. This has created the proverbial burning platform for the introduction and development of many new technologies that will drive a new era of the industrial revolution over the next 30 years. As well as tightening environmental legislation, increasingly companies will self

---

[3] From Bill Gates 1995 book "The Road Ahead"

regulate in the competition for the green pound. The term green pound relates to sales received as a result of business activity to improve sustainability and combat global warming.

Legal - health and safety, equal opportunities, advertising standards, consumer rights and laws, product labelling, product safety and environmental legislation detailed above. It is clear that companies need to know what is and what is not legal in order to trade successfully. If an organisation trades globally this becomes a very tricky area to get right as each country has its own set of rules and regulations. Falling foul of the law can have a significant detrimental impact on your business and so as well as serving and anticipating the needs of your customers, you need to ensure that you keep up to speed and compliant with all the latest legal requirements that relate to your business and the markets in which it operates. The introduction of the General Data Protection Regulations (GDPR) in 2018 has transformed they way in which companies can use data about a living person and this will change the way you are able to market and contact your customers as this has now got to be expressly authorised at the individual level.

The Strategy Canvas

In their brilliant 2005 book, Blue Ocean Strategy W. Chan Kim and Renée Mauborgne came up with a very simple but effective strategy canvas that gives an at a glance understanding of your product and service offering relative to the competition. The power lies in its simplicity and can be created quickly in a group session to get a clear understanding of the competitive landscape. The whole idea around the development of the Blue Ocean Strategy is not just to look at incremental improvements over the competition but to find a blue ocean where your competition becomes irrelevant. Marginal differences in your service offering relative to the competition are described as red ocean or shark infested!

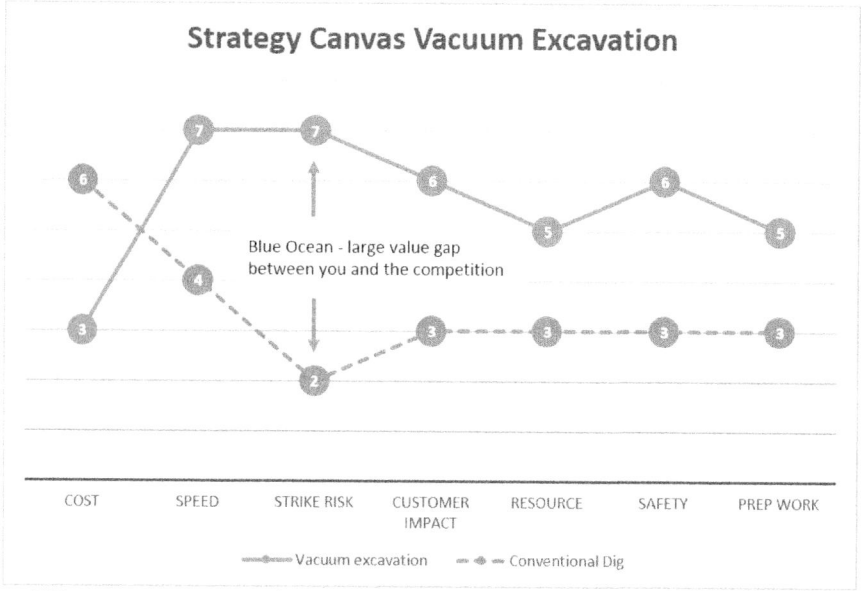

Figure 5 The strategy canvas and search for blue oceans

The strategy canvas above is for the use of a vacuum excavation machine over a conventional digger product. The vacuum excavator is a very powerful vehicle mounted vacuum cleaner that literally sucks up the muck and spoil to dig holes in the road to expose utility services. It has a significant advantage over a conventional digger as it is non intrusive and does not need to strike to dig. These were first introduced in 2006 in the UK when utility service strikes were a major problem for the utility maintenance industry costing the econmoy hundreds of millions per year in lost productivity and penalty fines.

The concept is simple with the value adding elements of the service along the X axis and the perceived benefit to the customer from low to high up the Y axis, you then simply score your own product or service offering against that of the competition. Again it is really important that the you are objective and grounded in reality at this point and wherever possible make sure that you have tangible evidence to support your assumptions. The scoring is subjective so it is all really about understanding where there are only marginal differences between you and the competition and where significant differences exist or can be created to give you a competitive advantage. In the example above the widest gap represents the reduced strike risk of the vacuum excavation solution. As a point of clarification relating to cost, the scoring on the chart is from the perspective of the customer so a high cost of the service will score low and the lower cost solution will score high. Having completed the strategy canvas example at this point you would check your marketing strategy for this service to ensure it majors on the benefits of reduced strike risk and how when selling the service you can overcome resistance to the increased cost.

The power of the strategy canvas lies in not only identifying where the blue oceans (or widest gaps) lie between your service and the competition but this can also provide insight on whether to introduce new elements of the service that would be percieved as high value that that are not currently offered by the competition.

Raise, Create, Reduce, Eliminate (R.C.R.E)

To compliment the strategy canvas, W. Chan Kim and Renée Mauborgne came up with the raise, create, reduce, eliminate exercise. This I like because what often happens in the creation of strategy is a plan that results in additional workload and activity which is then subsequently piled onto already stretched resources. When businesses always view the introduction of a new strategy as doing more of the new stuff they want, without the regard for where the additional resources are going to come from this contributes significantly to the 70% failure rate. Actively looking to make room for raise and create initiatives by reducing and eliminating others that are no longer adding value is a powerful and often overlooked concept. Later in the book I will highlight the need for allocating sufficient time during the the execution phase so be as ruthless as you dare when considering what to reduce and eliminate. There may be systems and processes that feel like they are worthwhile but are not strategically important to your long term success and take up a disproportionate amount of time and resource relative to the value they add. The raise, create, reduce eliminate grid is essentially about the sustainable use of your business resources. Maintaining the discipline to focus on the the elements of work that are adding value and keeping the focus on the right things is also a great way to retain your talented people by stopping them becoming overworked and disillusioned with where the business is heading.

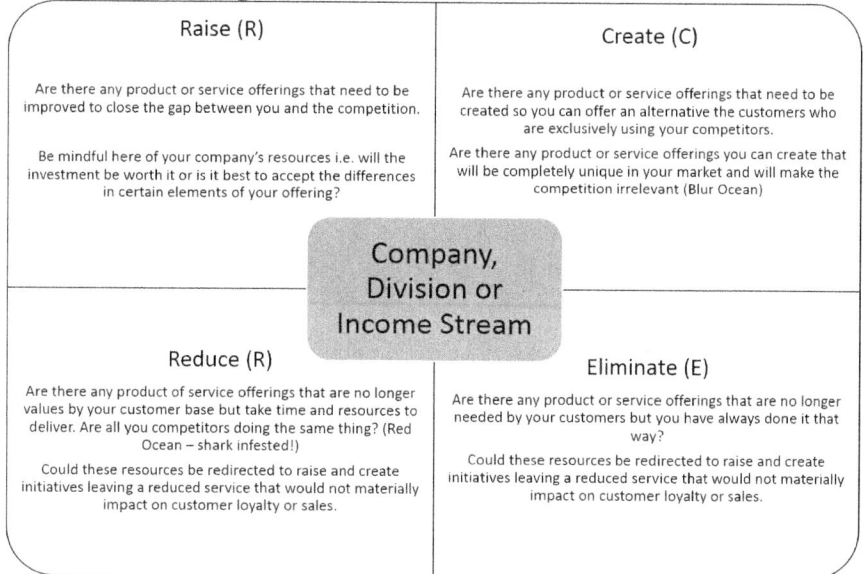

Figure 6 Raise, Create, Reduce, Eliminate (R.C.R.E)

Although I have introduced the R.C.R.E in the context of the value added service offerings for your customer, the tool is equally powerful when looking at your internal systems and processes. Applying the tool to your systems and processes may not directly change your customer offering but if the exercise results in streamlining and improving speed and cost by removing internal complexity, this can also be a great source of competitive advantage.

COMPETITIVE ADVANTAGE

Another powerful assessment tool which is similar to the Strategy Canvas and takes cognisance of your companies relative position to your competitors is the competitive advantage tool. This includes subjective scoring criteria against each element from 1 to 5 with 1 being the weakest and 5 being market leader. It is best to use this tool as a prompter for a group discussion as it will give real insight to the knowledge and confidence or lack of it from the rest of your team and highlight just how much intelligence you have on your competitors ability to compete against you.

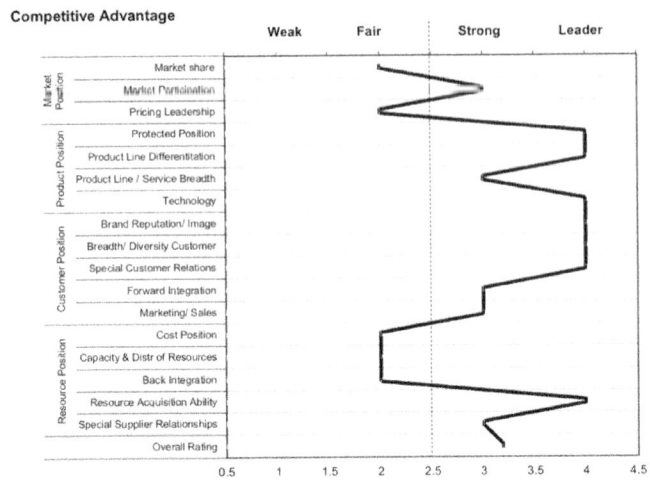

Figure 7 Competitive Advantage Model

Industry Attractiveness

Having established that you have a strong offering with the competitive advantage model it is also important to understand just how attractive the playing field is. This model can be a real bear trap and its worth a word of caution as generally the better a company is at doing something, the more bullish the participants will be about the attractiveness of their industry. The internet has been a massive disrupter to the traditional business models of many industries and without the right amount of diligence about what is actually happening, an organisation can realise when it's much too late to save itself. At the time of writing in the UK the online estate agency Purple Bricks is transforming the way people are buying and selling houses. Over the last few months when I have spoken to representatives of competing estate agents, I have yet to speak to any of them with a good word to say about the Purple Bricks business model but this could be a typical manifestation of initial competitor response. Throughout 2018 the industry was in a state of denial and as things get increasingly difficult they will either copy or die as the estate agency landscape goes the same way as insurance, home entertainment, banking, grocery shopping, clothes shopping, hotel booking, low cost airlines, dating and print media.

This model again includes subjective scoring criteria against each element from 1 to 5 with 1 being bad and 5 being excellent. Again use of this tool is best as part of a group discussion having completed the competitive landscape as these two models complement each other. The ideal output would be to have a strong competitive advantage in and attractive industry.

If however you have a strong competitive advantage in an unattractive industry, you must develop the conviction to collectively do something about it or face the consequences. With the invention of the electric light bulb by Thomas Edisson in the early 1900's, the new clean, instant lighting system soon began to be adopted. The gas lighting industry initially responded by re-doubling their efforts in a bid to compete and they did for a short period, before the superior lighting system was adopted. The gas lighting company with all its resources tried to compete in an unattractive industry (gas lighting) rather than invest in electrical street lighting, with all the competitive advantages you may have, you are doomed to failure if you market place changes and you are not prepared or able to do anything about it. If you are an estate agent reading this book, rather than explain away why you feel your service demands a premium over the online equivalent, maybe its time to rethink your business model.

Another dimension to analise when reviewing your indsutry attractiveness is to put yourself in your customers shoes and consider speed and availability of your service. In our 24 hour society it is not simply about being the best between 9am and 5pm Monday to Friday, you must also consider how flexible and availiable your product or service is to make it is truly attractive and therefore competitive to today's consumer.

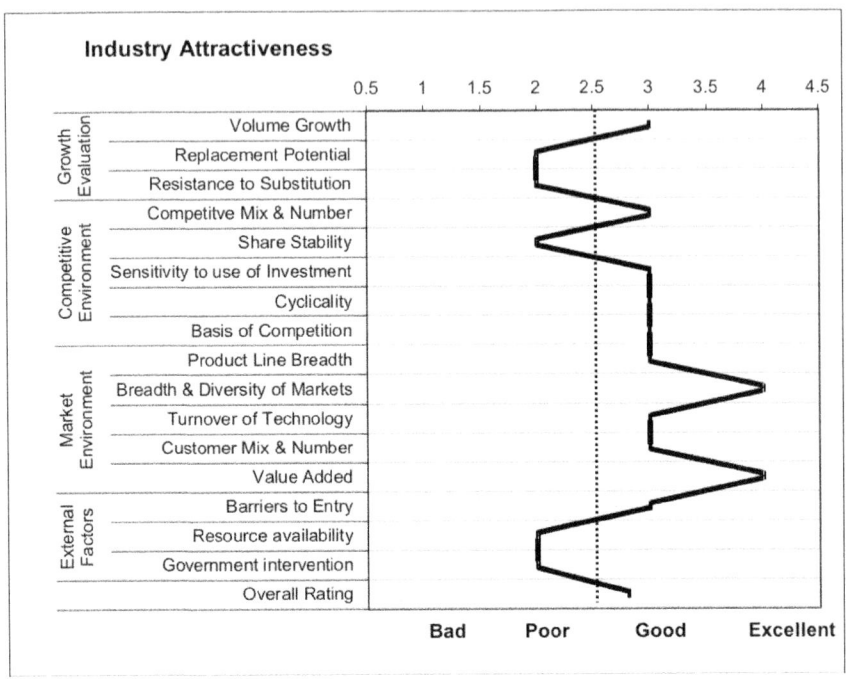

Figure 8 Industry Attractiveness

Once both tools have been completed the overall rating for competitive advantage and industry attractiveness can be fed into the tool below which is a simple four box grid giving an overall illustration of the offer position. The tool is also very useful if you have a number of different products or service streams because you can load them all in and get a great visual for the balance of your portfolio in terms of each revenue streams competitive advantage and industry attractiveness. Invariably your strongest products or services will be those driving the profit and cash through your business. If your best perfomer is in an a mature market place and facing the threat of demise or disrutive transformation (estate agents) then now is the time to use the profits from this revenue stream to

BUILDING A WINNING BUSINESS STRATEGY

reinvent yourself. It may sound radical but you should look for new ways to destory your own business before the competition does. If there was someone in the gas light industry that looked at their service as providing light, rather than providing gas light, then maybe they might have invented the electric lightbulb.

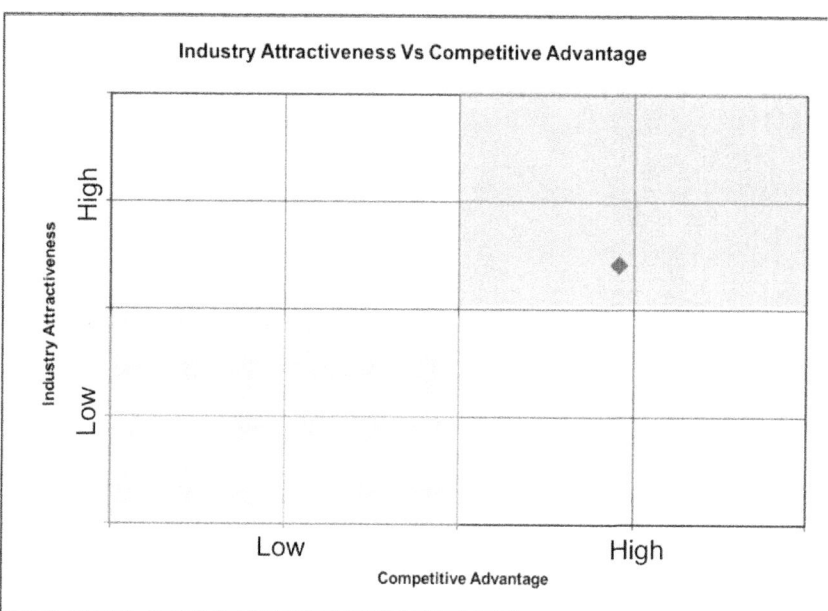

Figure 9 Industry Attractiveness and Competitive advantage

PRODUCT SERVICE LIFE CYCLE

Now you have established that you have a product or service with a competitive advantage in an attractive industry it is time to consider where you are in the product service lifecycle. If you are putting together a three to five year strategy, the maturity of the market for your offering may change considerably over the term of your plan and you may want to consider how you can adapt your plan to any foreseeable changes. If your strategy is to grow sales by 10% per year for the next 5 years but you are operating in a mature or declining lifecycle then this new business would have to be won at the expense of the competition in an increasingly competitive market. Alternatively your 10% sales growth ambition in the early stages of the lifecycle may well see you achieve the 10% year on year growth but still lose overall market share to the competition if they expand to take advantage of the growing market quicker than you do. When setting sales targets it is important to consider your targets dependency on competitive advantage, market attractiveness and the lifecycle stage of your product or service. If you have a well balanced portfolio of products and services it would be over-simplistic to state that you want to grow all sales by 10% as this would be near impossible for some of your offerings and decidedly under ambitious for others.

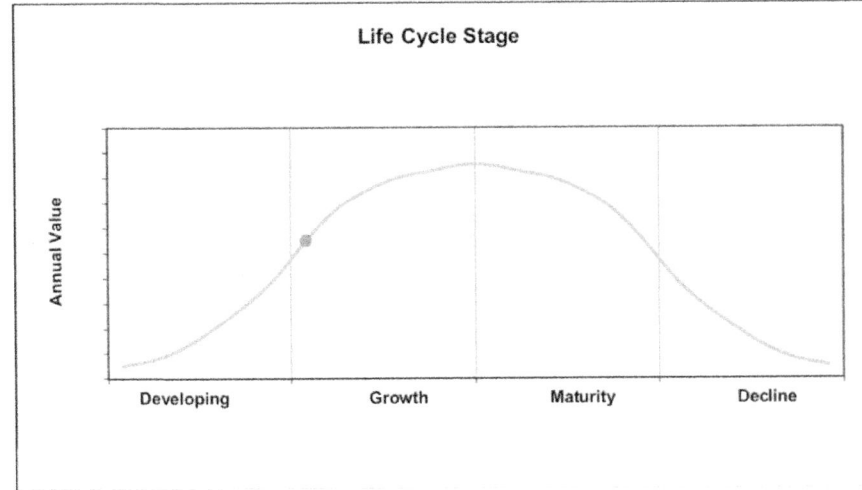

Figure 10 The four stages of the product lifecycle

As an example of a product life cycle, in the early 1980's the marketplace for uPVC double glazed windows was in its infancy. At that time there were just over 20 million homes in the UK that were fitted with wooden single glazed windows. The uPVC windows had significant advantages as they were warmer, had better noise reduction properties, were maintenance free and would last considerably longer than their wooden maintenance heavy counterparts. For the first 20 years the market for uPVC windows was in rapid growth as they became the must have home improvement product and the industry grew quickly. Today just over 30 years later the industry is in a state of maturity in the UK with significant consolidation in the provider base. In the case of uPVC windows the market will most likely plateau rather than decline as the UK needs to build 300,000 new homes a year until 2027 to keep pace with expected population growth. In this mature market the major players will be fighting for market share where any growth in their sales would come at the expense of the competition. The case for uPVC windows is a good example that played itself out over a 30 year timeframe which is way outside the parameters of most strategic plans. There are however industries with a much shorter lifecycle that may grow and decline over a five year strategic plan where a greater understanding of the position on the lifecycle would be of significant strategic importance. Over the next five years in the UK, the energy suppliers have committed to converting domestic customers on to smart metering for their energy services. There are companies that specialise in the installation of these meters that will be planning for double digit sales growth as they chase growing market volumes to meet demand. In this particular case the lifecycle curve would be a near perfect representation of the sales profile of a smart metering installer over the next five years. It may well be that the company plans for the lifecycle and structures its labour force, overheads and sales predictions accordingly. However it is all to common to see strategic plans that simply grow and grow off into the distance with little consideration of how the market will grow, evolve and in some cases predictably decline. Another similar example is the electric vehicle charging market in the UK which is expected to grow rapidly over the next 5 years, this again will see considerable investment and growth as the number of public charging points will explode from circa 16,000 to over 1 million in a very short timeframe. In planning for this growth as an EV charging point installer, you must also consider the likelihood that towards the end of your 5 year plan, the UK will be at near saturation point and consideration must be given to how you can transform and reinvest in your business to ensure its long term survival past the initial installation phase.

THE BOSTON CONSULTING GROUP (BCG) MATRIX

Another useful model for looking at the attractiveness of your product service offering is the BCG matrix. It is particularly powerful if you have a portfolio of products and services and you want an at a glance visual of where each revenue stream sits in your sales armoury and where you should invest resources or look at research and development to ensure life extension or the creation of new products to keep the balance healthy for the long term. If you are lucky enough to have some cash cow products in a mature market this is an ideal time to re-invest the cash in new products or services to strengthen the offer mix for the longer term. Many companies fumble away the advantages of the cash cows by thinking that these will be there forever without adequately anticipating their eventual decline with replacement product lines. Innovative companies such as 3M have policies where 15% of their employees time can be allocated to whatever pet innovation projects the employees want to work on. To put this in context, image being told that you can spend 6hrs of your 40hr working week exploring and developing any new product that you are interested in for the company. This insures that 3M have a long term sustainable pipeline of new ideas and innovation. They also have policies about generating 30% of income from products that are less than five years old. This deliberate and focussed strategy of essentially making their own products obsolete is part of 3M's culture and is also what has made it such a long term success. It is far better to replace your own products with something better than to wait for the competition to do it.

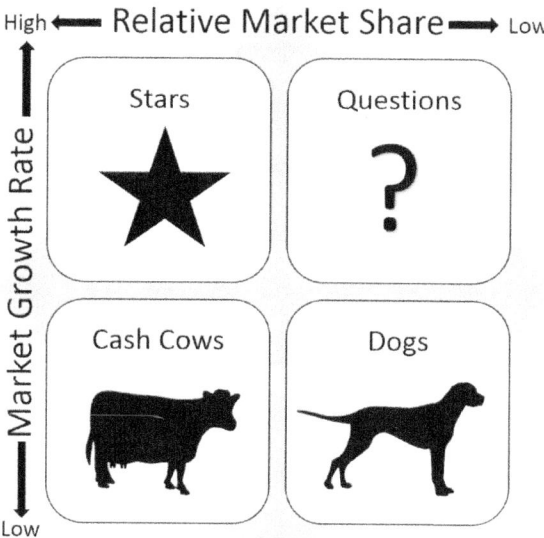

Figure 11 BCG Matrix 1970

Cash Cows – these face less competitive pressure along with low growth in market. These products do not require too much support and are dominant in their market enjoying a strong position achieved through economy of scale. The correct course of action with cash cows is to reinvest their income wisely. The history books are littered with companies that had cash cows and milked them all the way up the hill and down the other side.

Stars – these are fast growth and market leading products. A lot of investment is needed for these products to retain their position and maintain their lead over the competition to ensure future growth.

Question Marks – they usually have less market share in a dominant growing market. The product team need to decide whether to upgrade the product or discontinue it.

Dogs – these products have weak share in a low growth market. They are often responsible for making losses in a portfolio and should be discontinued. The potential exception to this is if these "dog" products are an enabler for customers to buy more of your premium related products, in these cases they could be considered a strategic hold to prevent customers going elsewhere.

When using the BCG matrix you will find that just by using the categorisation to place your products and service objectively, you will be having the right kind of constructive dialogue in your team that many companies seldom face into until its too late. The people on your team working on question marks and dogs are generally the last to admit it, herein lies the problem in many businesses where politics and personalities get in the way of making the right decisions at the right time for the right reasons. When managers invest their ego's in turning something around rather than having the courage and conviction to let something go, this is where you need a strong leadership team that holds each other to account and is not afraid to have the difficult conversations with one another.

We will cover values and culture later in the book but perhaps the greatest test of the values and culture of an organisation is when it is being challenged to make difficult and unpopular decisions. The function of leadership is not about trying to be everyone's friend or maintain the status quo, its about ensuring the long term success of the business and continued employment for the majority of its employees. The dogs and the question marks need to be adressed and the difficult decisions need to be made.

Porter's Five Force Analysis

In 1980 Michael Porter changed the landscape in terms of how organisations look at themselves and how they strategically assess their position and compete in the marketplace. The "five forces model", expands the users thinking away from the more obvious focus on direct competition and addresses where the power lies between the various stakeholders in the commercial relationship.

BUILDING A WINNING BUSINESS STRATEGY

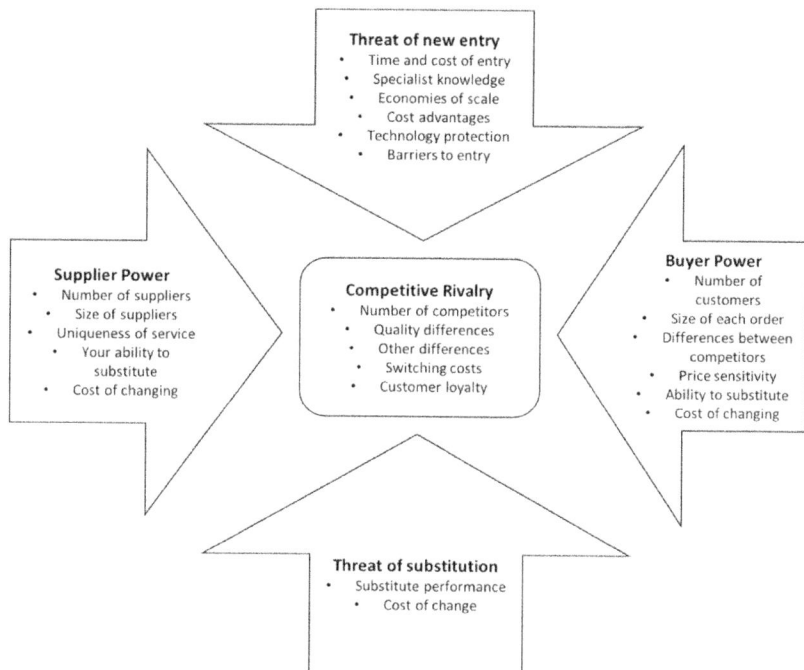

Figure 12 Michael Porter Five Forces of Competitive Advantage 1980

The formulation of strategy is about achieving a competitive advantage and this is not neccessarily always about being better, its also about being unique. To give your marketing and sales teams a chance, you need to give them a story worth telling about why your company is different and in a good way. The Porter model illustrates the five fundamental forces at play:-

1. **Threat of entry** – this is when new entrants compete for market share within an industry. Threat of entry is dependent on the barriers to entry which could be technology, legislation and licensing, as well as high capital investments required to get started.
2. **Intensity of rivalry** – this is all about the struggle that exists for market position. Price competition, technology innovation, marketing, customer service and warranties.
3. **Substitute products** – these are products from outside industries that vie for the same customers. Thinking about substitute products in this way can throw up some unlikely competition which would be missed if you were doing a more

straight forward competitive assessment. An example would be Harley Davidson motorcycles competing with sports cars and motorboats. These are examples of high value luxury status symbols that are competing for the same wealthy customer who wants to make a bold statement by demonstrating their wealth (whilst having fun of course).
4. **Bargaining power of buyers** – a limited number of buyers in the market can drive the competition with the bargaining for higher quality services and pitching the competitors against each other. The rail industry in the UK is an example of significant buyer power with Network Rail being right at the top of the food chain for all activity on the UK's rail infrastruture. As an incredibly powerful buyer, Network Rail makes sure that it keeps a healthy mix of competition in its supply chain to keep quality and prices under control.
5. **Bargaining power of suppliers** – a limited number of suppliers can threaten to raise prices or reduce quality to squeeze additional profitability from the marketplace.

The combination of the Five Forces determines the ultimate competitiveness of the industry. When Porter put his Five Forces model together in 1980, this was a full 10 years before computer scientist Tim Berners-Lee invesnted the World Wide Web which added a significant new dimension and disrupted the competitive landscape across just about every industry sector.

The Ansoff Matrix

As part of your strategy you may well be looking at expanding your product or service offering to grow sales, particulary if you have completed the industry attractiveness matrix. The Ansoff Matrix is a powerful 4 box grid that addresses the different dimensions of sales expansion to give the user insight into the associated challenges and risks. It is powerful when used along with the S.W.O.T analysis and Porters Five Forces as these models will complement the matrix to identify areas of strength and the potential paths of least risk and resistance to sales growth.

BUILDING A WINNING BUSINESS STRATEGY

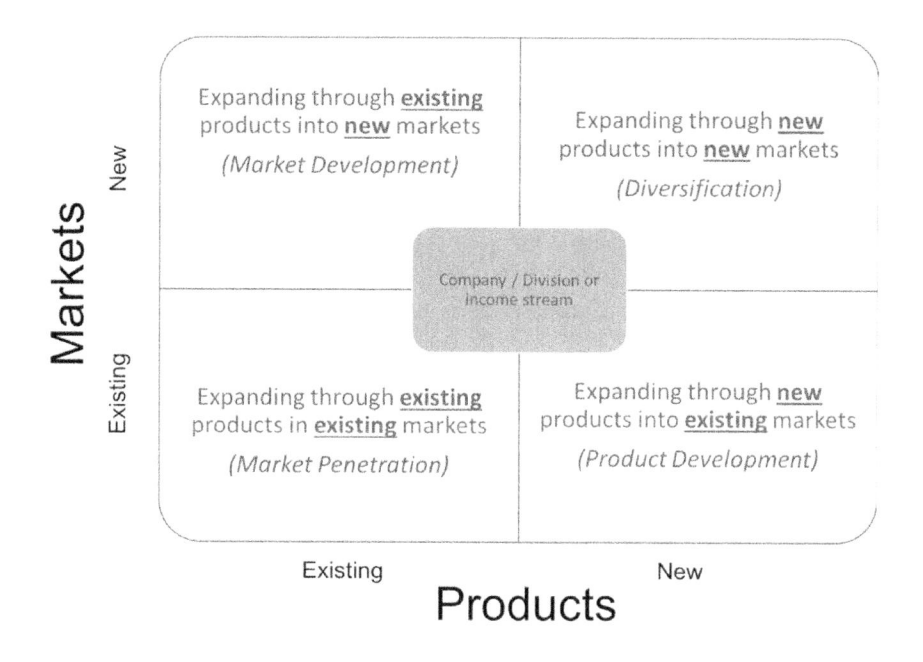

	Existing	New
New	Expanding through **existing** products into **new** markets *(Market Development)*	Expanding through **new** products into **new** markets *(Diversification)*
Existing	Expanding through **existing** products in **existing** markets *(Market Penetration)*	Expanding through **new** products into **existing** markets *(Product Development)*

Centre: Company / Division or Income stream

Markets (vertical axis) / Products (horizontal axis)

Figure 13 The Ansoff Matrix

Market Penetration - This is generally considered the easiest way to sales expansion as relationships and knowledge of your offering are already understood. To increase the wallet share of your existing customers you could consider increasing quality, productivity and marketing activity. Often the launch of a new strategy to grow sales is focused on new customers without fully understanding the complete needs and requirements of the existing customer base. A couple of years ago we did some analysis on our existing customers to understand just how much they had to spend on our product annually. With one particular customer we were doing £300,000 a year and we were confident that this was equal to or very near their budgeted spend. After making enquiries we learnt that their spend budget was closer to £1M a year. This was really useful as it started the dialogue on what we needed to do to get more wallet share (i.e a greater share of the customers availiable spend). Many sales people seem reluctant to ask their customers what their annual spend is but asking these kind of questions can give you powerful insight and reduce your dependency on using valuable resource and time adopting a more risky strategy to grow sales with new customers.

Make sure you are fully selling into your existing customers before you go looking elsewhere.

Market Development – More risky than market penetration, this may mean moving into a new geography and new customers who are currently being served by the competition. Apart from a potentially aggressive competitor response you have to overcome switching resistance in the customer base by investing in building new relationships through sales, marketing and business development. If you have done your strengths homework relative to the competition, make sure you are pushing the right message and engaging with your potential new customers in the right way. As an example if you have developed a product that can save your customers money but the purchase price is a little more expensive than the competition, then you need to be ready to handle the obvious cost objections by selling on value rather than discounting your costs. Developing your market through discounting a value adding product can be satisfying in the short term but not achieve and deliver on your strategy in the medium to long term.

Product Development – more risky than market penetration but in some cases the product development may well be as a result of customer feedback on product requirements. Responding to your customer base in this way can gain you favour as a supply chain partner who is willing to innovate. Be careful not to be completely customer led for all your innovation. Henry Ford once said that if he had asked his cutomers what they wanted they would have asked for a faster horse. True innovation is also about anticipating your customers unmet and future needs. James Dyson invented the bagless vacuum cleaner out of frustration whilst he was "Hoovering". The vacuum market used to compete on the size and power of their motors and how close they could get to the corners of your room but all of the availiable products at that time worked in much the same way with a rapid deteriation in suction power as the dust bag filled up and made the product very inefficient. The manufacturers relied on a healthy aftersales revenue stream of dust bags that none of them had the appetite to self canibalise by developing their own bagless cleaner. Dyson introduced a superior more expensive product that became an iconic status symbol and transformed the market. Dyson approached all of the major vacuum cleaner manufacturers with his cyclone bagless idea which they rejected out of hand. He eventually remortgaged his house and transformed the industry with a far more expensive but superior product (it can be done).

Diversification – This is by far the most risky route to new sales. The business history books are littered with companies that have done very well and then moved too far away from their core service offering or expertise. The rewards can be great and the challenges are not unsurmountable but you would be wise to consider first the other three expansion alternatives in order of risk. When considering diversification a key consideration should be adjacency, look for products, services or markets that are adjacent in many ways to your current offering. As well as considering the similarities that exist to your core competancies make sure you fully understand the differences as ultimately it will be how you deal with the differences large and small that will determine the success of your diversification strategy. Diversifying into a new offering that is 80% similar to your current activity may seem like unquestionable odds but proceed with extreme caution. Often when looking at ways to diversify leadership teams will overplay the similarities to the current core activity and down play the differences. Remember that human beings are 80% genetically similar to cows[4] and sometimes the 20% of differences can literally make all of the difference.

Figure 14 When considering diversification it's not about the similarities it's about the obvious and not so obvious differences.

STRATEGIC CHOICES

Strategy is about making choices and so far I have described how the discovery phase tools can be used to understand which course of action would be favourable over another dependent on strengths and weakness, market competitiveness and industry attractiveness. Once this piece of work has been completed you will have built a much clearer understanding on what your business should be focusing on in delivering the strategic plan. Thinking once again about the clarity of the selling of the strategy to everyone in the business and giving everyone a clear understanding of the choices made, it is also worth taking time to explain what the organisation is willing to say "No", too. Often a CEO will reveal a target for sales growth but without being specific enough about the strategic choices as mentioned in the earlier chapter. When this happens the sales team will sell anything the customer is willing to buy from them and companies get into difficulty as they start to move away from their core expertise in pursuit of new revenues to support the sales targets. In order to ensure there is real clarity, the model below is useful as it clearly articulates what your business is willing to say no to.

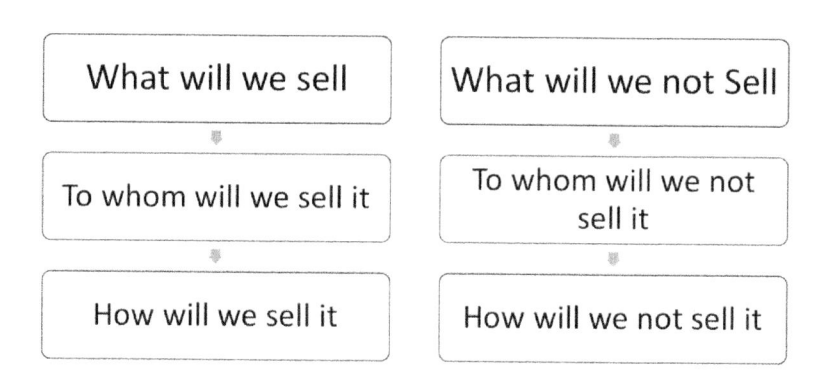

What will we sell	What will we not Sell
To whom will we sell it	To whom will we not sell it
How will we sell it	How will we not sell it

Figure 15 Strategic choices clarification - what you are willing to say "No" too.

"After a business implements a strategy, competitors will react, and the firm's strategy will need to adapt to meet the new challenges. There is no stopping point and no final battle. The competitive cycle continues on perpetually. Produce and compete or perish" —Thomas Timings Holme

If you have clarified your strategic choices in this way your teams can use this a guide over the coming months and years to ensure there is no drift in what you are willing to say yes and no to. To avoid being part of the 70% strategic failure club, you need to stay true to your core ideologies and only change your choices following a review of the right kind of changing circumstances. Using the strategic choices as a roadmap on how you are going to deliver £100M in sales is far better than just saying you want £100M in sales. In both cases you may well end up with £100M in sales but the profit margins, cash and long term sustainability of the business will be in a much better place with the additional guidance of the right strategic choices.

[iiii] Porter, Michael E. (1980). *Competitive Strategy.* Free Press. ISBN 0-684-84148-7.

4 Competitive Strategies

"You can have anything you want – you just can't have everything you want"—
Anonymous

Having a competitive strategy is very important as it defines what your company stands for and what you want to be famous for across your customer base. This is important as it communicates the values and ideology of your organisation to both your customers, potential employees and your partners. As you consider ways in which you can grow your business, the key to long term success is to hold true to your companies ideology and what the brand stands for. In his brilliant book "Built to Last", Jim Collins studied 18 extraordinary companies which had enjoyed enduring success. One of his key findings was that companies that preserve their core ideologies while relentlessly stimulating progress and improvement are the ones that significantly outperform the competition over the long term. He identified three general strategic approaches:-

Overall cost leadership – This is only a viable strategy if you have the lowest operational costs in your industry. Companies like Southwest Airlines, Ryanair, Aldi and Lidl supermarkets have defined themselves as cost leaders and use this strategy to obtain market share and scale volume to keep their unit cost base low. This is great from a customer's perspective but a relentless pursuit of cost cutting and efficiency needs to be maintained overtime. When Argos catalogue was launched in the UK in 1972 its main competition was other catalogues such as Kays and Gratton (pre internet printed catalogues for household goods offering weekly payment terms and very popular with working class households) that were significantly more expensive as they charged a premium for extended payments and home delivery. The Argos business model with self-collection, superior inventory management, and efficient use of store/warehouse space won customers based on cost leadership from the more expensive home delivery catalogues of the time. Some 45 years later the Argos name has survived the recession but has lost its original appeal around cost leadership and its recent acquisition by Sainsbury in 2016 has seen it co-locate in the supermarkets stores to save on cost whilst improving it's logistics operation to compete with Amazon. Hindsight is a wonderful thing but why did Argos not grow and develop into Amazon? A truly relentless pursuit of a cost leadership ideology may well have filled the space that Amazon ultimately occupied. Instead when Amazon launched in 1995 the competition far from seeing them as a threat, practically ridiculed the business model and for the first six years they had good reason to. It took Jeff Bezos six years to post his first profitable quarter but by the end of 2017, what is left of the competition and the media is now silenced and Mr Bezos is the richest man in the world. Today you cannot have a strategy of cost leadership in retail if you have any physical store presence and this presents a significant problem for high street retailers who are playing out their strategies quiet literally on the wrong playing field.

Differentiation – this approach is used where a company stands out by creating a product or service that is perceived to be unique in the industry. This is very similar to the concept of a Blue Ocean strategy where the competition becomes irrelevant. One good example is the Nintendo Wii which at the time of launch was the first games consoles to use interactivity which tackled the perception of computer gameplay as being a sedentary solitary pastime and created a whole family user base that people would play sociably at parties. The Nintendo Wii used a lower cost graphics chips but unlike the Microsoft XBox and the Sony PlayStation the Wii did not have to compete on the performance of the microprocessor. At its launch it was the only console that offered the interactivity along with game play and enjoyed a couple of years in the calm blue ocean that it had deliberately created.

Focus – a company will zoom in on a particular buyer group, type of product or geographic market. Using this approach a focused company can obtain leadership and a stronghold which makes it unattractive for potential market entrants to want to compete in a narrow field with a dominant provider. A good example here is Tetra Pak which is the Swedish producer of milk cartons and its pretty much all they have focused on since they made their first in 1952 which by 2017 it had earned the Tetra Laval group annual sales of £11.5Bn (a lot of milk cartons).

Some strategies are deliberate and some are emergent, some organisations talk about and plan strategy all the time and some organisations never mention or talk about strategy at all. The important thing to remember is that any organisation competing in an industry has a competitive strategy, whether explicit or implicit. Strategy in business is a little bit like gravity you can try and ignore it but it will not ignore you. You can have a very successful business without ever really thinking about or recognising your strategy but of course it will exist. Using the discovery phase toolkit in section 3 will provide you with the insight needed to ensure you fully understand what you need to do to protect your position if you currently have a successful strategy or what you might need to change if you want to improve the fortunes of your organisation from its current position.

Gaining insight and understanding of your strategic position will help you make the necessary choices. Remember good strategy is also about remembering to say "No" to any course of action that weakens your position and of course you can only do this if you know what your current position is. Remember to stick close to what makes you famous with your customers (sometimes refered to as your core business offering) and be true to your organisations ideology. This is ultimately how brands are built and when you steer off course this is how they can also be destroyed. When companies start trying to be all things to all people they are in danger of ending up in the mediocre middle. Woolworths was unique when it was founded in 1909 as it was the first "walk around store", which encouraged customers to browse as opposed to the conventional wisdom at the time that assumed that all customers knew exactly what they wanted when they entered the store and were immediately presented with a counter and shop assistant. Woolworths either deliberately or inadvertently stumbled upon that part of our personality as a shopper that does not realise that we needed something until we have seen it. Woolworths was a great brand and was the symbolism of towns up and down the UK with over 750 stores nationwide. It could be argued successfully that Woolworths became a victim of the internet but it had also lost its way in terms of how it defined itself to the customer and as a store it ended up in the mediocre middle where its ranges were too broad. For example it was stocking more than 40 types of pencil case. It was in the middle on records and DVD's, HMV was better. It was in the middle on children's toys, Toys R Us was better, it was a leader on pick n mix and I'm struggling to remember what else Woolworths did but then I guess that is the point I'm trying to make here.

5 The build phase

"Strategy is not the consequence of planning, but the opposite: it's the starting point."
— Henry Mintzberg

So having taken the time to think deeply about and fully understand your competitive position and where each of your products and services meets your customers current and future needs, you are now in a position to build the strategy.

The CEO will now be getting impatient as she has already told everyone that the strategy is to grow sales to £100m over the next 5 years. By now I hope you realise that this is not a strategy it's just a goal and this goal may not be able to be achieved without jeopardizing the long term success of the organisation. So often when five year strategic plans are put in place, two much of the emphasis is placed on the financial position at some fixed point 3 or 5 years into the future without any regard for what happens afterwards. Building great companies and strategy is about the long game and playing the long game based on the organisations core ideology, skills and expertise. The key to building a sustainable strategy is to make sure that all of the components are in place and the competing business improvement initiatives are well balanced. For example if you are purely aiming for a short term financial goal of improving profit, you could stop investing in training, development and investment in new systems. This short term view would potentially jeopardise the long term success of the organisation. So the key to building a sustainable business is to make sure all of the necessary building blocks are in place. Robert S. Kaplan and David Norton developed the concept of the balanced scorecard in 1991, which tackled the problems associated with too much focus on pure financial measures. I will come onto the use of the Balanced Scorecard and its benefits later in the book. To compliment the creation of the balanced scorecard they developed the strategy map, I think this is an excellent example of how to build a strategy with the audience in mind. As mentioned in the earlier section, the most fundamental part of the strategic process is the execution phase and immediately prior to the execution phase comes the launch and the communication. Having a strategy map that can be explained almost as a story with a beginning, middle and an end is a great way of getting buy in and understanding of what the strategy is going to achieve, how it will be achieved and what's in it for the people of the organisation. Applying a storylike commentary to your strategic process is a very good way of making it stick as storytelling has been used across all cultures for thousands of years as a way of sharing and disseminating information. The hearts and minds selling of the strategy needs to focus on more than just getting to £100M of sales and 10% net operating profit. The people who get excited by financial goals are the CEO, CFO, anyone that receives a bonus on the financial results and the shareholders. If this does not apply to everyone in your organisation like for example in the John Lewis partnershp, then you need to identify other more compelling ways in which to sell the strategy and the financial goals in a way which resonates more closely with the majority of the people in the business.

The strategy map is an ideal tool for the creation of a sustainable strategy that addresses the needs of all stakeholders and not just the shareholders. To some it would feel counter intuitive to create a strategy map to achieve the CEO's financial challenge as the main focus of the strategy map is on just about everything else but the finances. This seemingly paradoxical approach recognises that you cannot improve the finances of the organisation over the long term without improving everything else first. Cost cutting to improve profit is like crash dieting, where short term success can be quickly lost and in some cases lead to a worsening of the position over the longer term. Other quick fixes to improve finances like reduced quality or reduced sales and marketing activity will inevitably create a legacy of potential problems to support the future sales pipelines. Leadership teams that do not fully address the needs and balance of all the stakeholders are simply sacrificing long term success for short term results. At this point you may be reading this book and thinking, yes this is all well and good but I need to do something quickly to improve the financial position in my organisation and now it looks like this strategy map is more of a long game that only starts to improve the financial position after everything else. Well you will be pleased to know that in fact the strategy map is every bit as efficient at delivering speedy results as some of the more draconian measures and short cuts. The reason for this is that it is clear, there's something in it for everyone and it will galvanise your entire workforce into positive action. The first time I was introduced to the strategy map and balanced scorecard was in a turnaround situation. The CEO at the time faced a lot of internal criticism for its introduction when the operational teams thought it was a waste of time and we should simply concentrate on cutting costs. The resulting improvements in both the finances and the operational performance of the company gave our financial backers the confidence to stick with us and it ultimately saved the organisation which was at one point only hours away from collapse. First let's take a look at a typical strategy map and then I will explain the benefits of the approach.

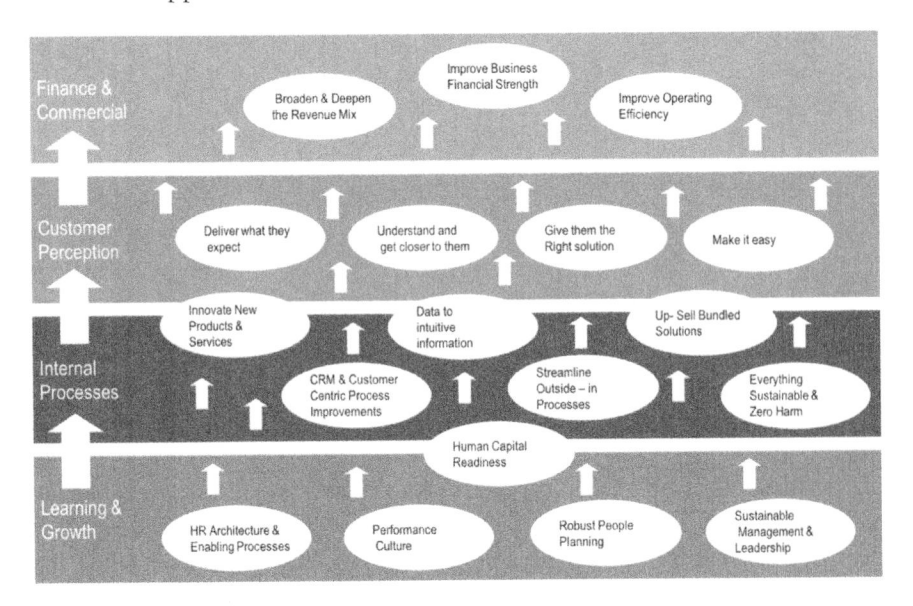

The layers of the strategy map are split into four distinct areas of performance that are aligned to the resulting Balanced Scorecard. The order of the layers are significant as the strategy map is a cumulative build of performance that improves the long term financial health of the business as a result.

Learning and Growth

The learning and growth section is all about human capital readiness or overall people capability for short. This is all about having the right people in the right roles, with the right skills and competence with the right objectives aligned to the overall goals or strategy of the organisation. This layer is at the bottom but it is what I would call the foundation layer of the organisation and you cannot build a successful long term strategy without getting this right. So many senior leaders will say that people are our greatest asset but then under invest in learning and growth in the pursuit of short term profitability. The aspects of the strategy map in learning and growth should all be aimed at achieving employee engagement in the strategy. Employee engagement and motivation is a vast field of study that has had nearly as many books written about it as strategy so in the next chapter I will go into more detail on for me what is the most important part of any successful strategy and that's getting the people part right.

The learning and growth section is not just the concern of the human resources team, it should be a fundamental shared objective of all managers to make sure the processes are followed and active consideration is given to organisation and job design, resourcing levels, clarity of objectives, opportunities for growth, advancement and meaningful market competitive reward and recognition. Managers should be trained and developed on giving balanced and appropriate feedback with ongoing refinement as well as adequately being able to face into disputes and conflict resolution. Developing high performing teams is by far the most difficult aspect of all leadership endeavours and its importance cannot be over-estimated. All great companies that perform over the long term have strong leadership and cultures at their heart. The problem is that there are no hard and fast rules for how winning cultures should be built and maintained but later in the book we will look at the buiding blocks for employee engagement which need to be attended to.

Internal Processes

The internal process part of the strategy map is concerned with making sure that your people are working with expert systems and processes. Increasingly the use of technology can be used as a source of competitive advantage so the organisation must make sure that the right kind of investment is made in the supporting infrastructure to enable your people to perform at their best. Having an understanding of how you are going to compete in the marketplace can drive investment in your processes to deliver your key advantages over the competition. Going back to the Walmart example, Walmart would be willing to open stores in locations that were not considered viable by their larger and more well established rival K-Mart. Both K-Mart and Walmart started using bar code technology in their stores at he same time in the early 1980's but Walmart made better use of the data by networking all their stores and standardising their product range based on buyer behaviour. Kmart on the other hand ran each of its stores almost independently of each other and local store managers were responsible for product choice and inventory. K-Mart wrongly assumed that they had a scale advantage by only opening stores in local populations of greater than 100,000 people but Walmart through its smarter systems and processes had a much greater scale advantage as every store in the country was networked so the supply chain could be leveraged at a national rather than local level which enabled the cost leadership position for Walmart and K-Marts ultimate and with hindsight, almost inevitable demise. Having the very best talented and engaged people in your organisation can only get you so far, these people also need expert systems and processes to compete effectively by doing the basics brilliantly. At the time when Walmart started to network its stores this was more to do with their core ideology of serving the customer by anticipating and stocking for their needs but this represents a near perfect example of how expert people and expert systems can improve customer perception and drive loyalty.

Customer Perception

This is about delivering the customer experience, if you are going for cost leadership then of course your customers will have a very tangible way of measuring if you have got this right. The internet has been a great leveller in making pricing information ubiquitous to all. Your customers are only a google search and 0.01seconds away from establishing whether or not you are indeed a cost leader. If you are going for customer service as a differentiator, then you have to make sure that the customer experience is designed and consistent. Many companies talk about exceeding customers expectations and this is a common pitfall as they are not explicit enough with their employees what the customers expectations are and how to exceed them. If each individual is empowered in your organisation to exceed the customers' expectations, this can be a very dangerous approach, especially if a key part of your strategy is based on exceptional customer service. If you are going to compete on customer service you must design the customers experience so that it is consistent, otherwise you will exceed their expectations on Monday when employee A provides the service and fall short of their newly created expectations on Tuesday when employee B serves them. Perhaps one of the best examples of customer service consistency is McDonalds where they have gone to great detail to systematise the service delivery experience to the point where you can go to anyone of their 30,000 restaurants in over 100 countries and get the same customer experience. If you are going to have a policy of exceeding the customers expectations, then you have to design in that additional experience and make it consistent. For example many hotels now offer pillow menu's as a differentiator, which when first experienced will exceed the weary travellers expectations but then this will become associated as the norm and thus rasing the bar for what new and innovative ways will be developed to create the pleasant and unexpected customer experience on their return visit.

Another common pitfall when designing a customer experience is that companies do not consider the whole purchase to pay lifecycle when designing their service offering. Unless you create a consistent experience at all points of contact with your customers, this can damage and erode any good work that your employees are doing in delivering the service. As an example if you are a plant hire company and you have spent a lot of money on marketing and selling a superior customer service experience where you make sure the equipment is delivered to your customer on time, you have provided the customer with all of the user and safety information, the equipment is in good clean working condition, at the end of the hire period you collect the equipment on time and leave the customer with a collection note. At this point you have a very satisfied customer who would more than likely give you that all important repeat business. Then your accounts department sends the customer an esoteric invoice that he cannot understand and the account goes unpaid and disputed for months on end causing unnecessary friction between your respective companies. Companies that really appreciate and are careful to design the full end to end customer experience spend as much time and effort designing their invoices as they do their marketing materials. People will remember the worst part of your service and invariably this comes at the point at which companies request payment as they do not spend enough time designing something that is clear, concise and easily understood with no surprises. In these days of Trip Advisor, Feefo and Trust Pilot, extra care needs to be taken to ensure everyone of your customers stakeholders feels equally delighted at your level of service throughout that procurement to payment cycle (they all have a voice).

Financial and Commercial

This section is all about making sure you are making money, collecting cash and securing the long term financial stability of your business. In response to the CEO challenging the business to 10% year on year sales growth and an improvement in profit margins you have first of all fully considered your competitive position, chosen an appropriate strategy linked to your particular skills and core expertise. Then you have started to build the strategy map by making sure that you have the best people working on the best systems all designed to give your customers a deliberate and designed consistent customer experience. Generally if you have done this well enough, the financial aspects of your business will look after themselves. You do however need to make sure that you have the right financial governance in place to ensure that you protect your profit margins and cash flow. Things to consider for this part of your strategy is how you keep control of your costs and maximise your revenues. This sounds easy but you need to make sure that you have robust processes in place and delegated financial authorities to ensure that only people that are authorised to spend money and make commercial commitments on behalf of the organisation have the means to do so.

Electronic purchase order systems are ideal at controlling spend levels and separating the requestors and approvers as part of a well-controlled procurement system. The other advantages of an electronic system are that you can derive value from your supply chain by consolidating purchases with a limited number of suppliers to get the best deals. By spending more with fewer suppliers, not only will you secure greater discounts or rebates based on volume but you will have greater influence on your suppliers delivery and standards as the significance of your leveraged spend with them will move you further towards their top 10 customer list. If you remember back to Porters Five Forces model, effectively your customer buyer power inevitably increases as you leverage your spend with the supply chain. A lot of this book has been focussed on the unique offering into your customer base and how best to position yourself to win at the expense of the competition, but again all the hard work can be lost so make sure you also have a supply chain strategy that helps keep your costs under control whilst delivering your designed service to the customer. Depending on which type of industry you are in, your supply chain costs are generally second only in scale to your own labour costs and with the correct control this can mean the difference between a company that is struggling and one that is outperforming its peers in the market. I often get a little too excited about making sure we keep the costs under control but the following example illustrates the power of controlling your costs to improve your margins.

If your company makes 1.5% net operating profit and you can save £10,000 a year by consolidating and leveraging your supply chain. This means that going forward you would be able to do £666,666 less revenue to achieve the same financial result. I find it useful when talking about potential cost savings in this way because although £10,000 is a lot of money, the people in your business will have a healthy appreciation of just how difficult it is to sell, win and do £666,666. It is suprising how many people do not appreciate that saving £10,000 in this way it will drop straight through to the bottom line.

From a commercial perspective you need to make sure that supply terms and conditions are clearly understood and have been drafted in such a way as to remove or transfer as much risk as possible away from your organisation. Generally there are industry norms relating to commercial risk appetite and its about making sure that you are no more or less onerous than the competition unless of course you are using a commercially innovative model as a competitive advantage for your customers. Also to consider from a commercial perspective is cash flow and it's all about making best use of supplier payment terms and your own customer payment terms to try and achieve cash neutral or ideally cash positive activity where your customer payments finance your operations. So if your customers are paying you in 30 days and your suppliers are giving you 60 day payment terms this is preferable as it gives you a positive cash flow. Cash management is critically important to any business, so a thorough understanding of working capital requirements and a well drafted and enforced set of commercial conditions is of paramount importance. More companies go bust as a result of running out of cash than they do for running out of profit. Cash is the lifeblood of the organisation and should be treated as such.

Even though I have basically said that to improve the financial position of the business by concentrating first on just about everything else, it is very important that any increased sales you enjoy as a result of the meticulous planning of your strategy and customer service offering, does actually add economic value to your business i.e. you can make a profit. There is no point in having delighted customers and increased sales and then realizing that your cost of supply is greater than or too close to your sales revenue.

Now that you are making profit and gerating cash you will also need to consider ways in which you can reinvest your profits back into your business to help it grow.

6 Put your employees first

"To win in the marketplace you must first win in the workplace." –Doug Conant

The specifics of your own strategy, what you will compete on and how you will serve your customers will of course depend upon your industry and market sector so it would be near impossible for me here to try and cover off every possible scenario. What I can give more detail on however is the people side of your strategy. Irrespective of what sector you operate in and what your strategy is, you will have people in your business that have some basic needs that need to be met to keep them motivated and engaged in your business. The better you are at engaging your people, the more successful the organisation will become.

Some leaders talk about engagement and motivation almost interchangeably, but there are subtle differences. Motivation can be both carrot and stick and tends to be short term. Motivation looks at incentives and disincentives usually to reach or avoid a specific performance metric. Motivation is good in production line work with tangible measures of performance that can be incentivised and is more commonly associated with time and motion scientific methods of management. The concept of motivation has been around for many years but towards the latter part of the twentieth century the motivation movement shifted more towards employee engagement. Fifty years ago, financial incentives were a key motivator for production work and the average person had to work all week just to pay the bills and make ends meet. Nowadays even though it doesn't always feel like it we are comparably better off than the previous generation and so we are seeking much more from our working life than simply paying the bills. Consequently employers have to deliver on a much wider range of fulfillment needs to keep us truly engaged. The list below is taken from the Best Companies Employee engagement survey which is a national survey company and is responsible for producing the list of the Times Top 100 places to work in the UK. The best companies team split the engagement survey into 8 Factors :-

1. **My Manager** – they say that people join businesses and leave bad managers and so how an employee gets on with and respects their manager is one of the most significant determinants of how engaged an employee will be. Of all of the engagement metrics this is possibly the one with the greatest correlation of engagement. If you do not get on with your immediate line manager, it would be very difficult to achieve true engagement at work.
2. **My Team** – this looks at how supportive our teams are and if a good team relationship exists. Again if people feel part of a strong and genuine team, this can have a profound effect on how engaged they feel in their work.
3. **My company** – how a person feels about their company, are they proud to work there and are they proud of the work that the company does. Does the company have a strong social conscience and is it respected in it's industry with an enviable reputation.
4. **Leadership** – do employees feel that the leadership is taking the organisation in the right direction and leading with sound moral principles that uphold the companies values. Do employees feel valued by the leadership and feel free to have their say on aspects of work that affects them. Do the employees feel listened to and can they freely express their concerns and share ideas for improvement.
5. **Wellbeing** – increasingly the wellbeing performance area shows a strong correlation with overall engagement levels in the organisation. Does the organisation care for its employees, does it offer flexibility to fit around modern lifestyles, do the employees feel like their working environment and expectations that are placed on them by their employer, support their mental health and wellbeing.
6. **Personal Growth** – do employees have a clearly mapped out

career path and feel like their career aspirations are being met, do they feel that the organisation uses the best of their talents and works to actively develop them to achieve their full potential. Does the organisation actively manage and support their people's careers.
7. **Fair deal** – do employees feel like they get paid and treated fairly for the work that they do. Do the employees feel like they get paid fairly relative to other people in the organisation and similar organisations in the same industry. Is there equity and transparency in the rewards that are given for a job well done.
8. **Giving something back** – do employees feels like their organisation gives something back to the wider community and has a strong conscience of social responsibility. Do the employees get the opportunity to work in the community and support local charities.

Each of these 8 fFactors of engagement are responded to anonymously via a questionnaire sent to every employee in the organisation. The enlightened CEO's and very best organisations appreciate the power of engaged employees and the value of being able to tell prospective employees they have been recognised as an employer with a strong Employee Value Proposition (EVP). To attract and retain talent you have to meet or exceed all these requirements for the employee or face losing out to the competition. As the service economy continues to grow and represent an increasingly larger proportion of our economy, it's important to be able to attract great people. As even product based companies like McDonalds rely heavily on the supporting quality of service in product delivery.

To support and maintain an engaged workforce you also need to consider if your company has the right human resource systems and processes in place to ensure your people are enabled to do their best. As people are the means by which all strategy and performance is delivered I will again spend a little time in this section going through the systems and processes to support getting the right people into the organisation and keeping them there performing at their best. Below are the key building blocks and sequence to making sure you attract and retain the very best people:-

1. **Role Profile** – this is essentially the requirements of the role and should include a detailed description of what the post holder would be expected to do. This is the first and best opportunity you have to get the person you are looking for. A

common pitfall with role profiles is that they are absent or rushed and are not specific enough to enable a detailed screening process. Having worked in engineering I have often been surprised that managers will spend more time writing a detailed specification for a new tool in the workshop than they will a new person and yet getting the people specification wrong can turn out to be very costly as it is a significantly larger investment.

2. **Values & Behaviours** – as well as being able to identify people with the skills to do the activity detailed on the job description, you also need to ensure fit with your organisations culture and values. If you hire only for people that can do the job i.e. they have an engineering degree or they are a qualified accountant, you may well find that you hire the wrong personality into a previously harmonious team. Often people with specialist technical ability are in short supply but no hire at all is better than a bad hire. As you are reading this section you will probably be able to name at least one person in your organisation who is good at their job, but this comes at a heavy price as they leave a wake of disruption and disharmony that impacts on the engagement of the whole team. Of course it's not always possible to hire for attitude and train for skill but for many positions I would value cultural fit over technical ability.

3. **On-boarding** - Having selected the right person, it is important to make sure that you work hard to get the first day at work off to the best possible start. You only have one chance to make a first impression and if you are not careful you can destroy what I call the honeymoon period on day one. Common mistakes here include, equipment and building passes not being ready, the line manager unprepared and failing to make the new joiner feel welcome and introduce them to the wider team. The new starter gets put in a room on their own to watch the mandatory safety videos and or read through the company manual. This of course is essential but should be balanced with the new employee also being told about the company mission statement, values, receive an overview of the current challenges, get invited to any upcoming company events and get a good understanding from their line manager what will be expected of them through their probationary period. Take the time to put yourself in the new starters shoes and consider how they will respond to the questions from their family about their first day at work when they get home.

4. **Performance Reviews** – regular performance reviews should

take place ideally twice a year with more frequent informal reviews during 1:1's with employees and their line manager. At the beginning of each measurement period which is usually the financial year, the employee objectives should be set and aligned to contribute to the overall delivery of the strategy. The objectives should be Specific, Measureable, Achievable, Relevant and Timed (S.M.A.R.T.) so taking the CEO's ambition to grow sales to £100M over the term of the plan, this lofty goal needs to be broken down into specific actions. Below I have given some examples for a salesperson in this situation it may look something like this.

Not SMART – get closer to your key customers and grow sales year on year through existing and new accounts.

SMART Objective – achieve a sales target of £5M this financial year with an average sales increase of 10% across existing accounts and grow your new customer base by 10% whilst achieving a minimum profit margin of 12%.

As well as setting individual objectives you must also make sure that when the individual objectives are delivered, that you get the overall result you were looking for. A few years ago a business unit director that I was working with had been given a target of £5m sales for his area of the business. I found out as part of the performance review process that he had cascaded sales objectives to his sales team that only added up to £4M, which of course is not a recipe for success. To de-risk the overall target achievement, ideally he should have cascaded sales targets to achieve £6M to allow for any misses in performance of his sales team and consequently not jeopardising his business unit targets.

As well as setting S.M.A.R.T objectives you should also consider setting objectives that are related to the values of your organisation. In the absence of setting a clear expectation of values and behaviours you will end with people getting the right results but potentially going about it in the wrong way. Using poor behaviors to achieve results invariably ends up costing the company more in the long run.

5. **Succession Planning** – as personal growth is one of the key engagement factors, it is important that you have an active succession planning framework to ensure you have a pipeline of

talent for the key roles and positions in the organisation. Many companies either have an informal plan where the CEO has earmarked successors for key roles or they will have a plan but fail to let the individuals know that they are being considered for a future senior role. I have worked with business leaders who are reluctant to formalise the succession planning process as they prefer to keep everyone guessing and therefore trying harder or they are reluctant to share their plans with the individuals concerned through fear that they may take their foot off the gas. The art of good succession planning is to keep your plan flexible but make sure that the people on the plan know that you have recognised their potential future performance but it is by no means a pre-ordained rite of passage. When Jim Collins studied the 18 outstanding companies in built to last he found without exception that the most successful long running organisations obsessed about succession management planning. Many other companies that enjoyed blistering success with a rock star CEO, quickly faltered after their departure as they struggled to find appropriate replacements.

THE SUCCESSION MANAGEMENT TEMPLATE

Below I have mocked up an example of a simple succession management template. This gives a quick at a glance picture of any talent risk for key positions in the organisation.

	Managing Director	Sales Director	Operations Director	Engineering Director	Human Resource Director	Health & Safety Director	Finance Director
Current Holder	Fred Smith	Mike Lord	Jane Bradley	Peter Hanson	Mark Smith	Bob Hodge	Alison Pearce
Ready Now		Julie Pearce			Anita Low		
Emergency	Tom Walsh	Julie Pearce	External	External	Anita Low	Neil Smith	External
1-2 years	Tom Walsh	Andrea Harvey	External	Tracy Green	Anita Low	Neil Smith	External
3-5 years	Carl Hobs Clare Smith	Matt Lucas Trevor Smith	Carl Evans	Gerry Berry Tom Daley	Charlotte Farmer	Simon Lee Mark Evans	Debbie Hall

Figure 16 Senior Leadership Team Succession Management Grid

The table above has been produced for the senior team and in each of the rows beneath the current role holders, the potential replacements are named as successors.

Ready Now- Anyone who is classed as being ready now gives you an immediate and obvious successor to the current role holder. The challenge here is that these individuals may become a retention risk if their promotion does not come in the timescales to match their career ambition and expectations.

Emergency – The emergency candidates are the people that you would put into the role temporarily while a full time alternative can be found. They are have skills and competency to cover off the day to day requirements of the role but they may either be the wrong fit in terms of leadership style or they may ultimately be aspiring to a different permanent role and unwilling to take the role on as a permanent assignment.

1-2 Years – These are the people who need to be actively developed and given increased responsibility to prepare them for promotion within the next 1-2 years.

3-5 Years – These are the up and coming talented people that are potentially 3 to 5 years away. You will note that there may be more than one name in this box as it is healthy to have a strong pipeline of candidates to choose from.

External – wherever you have no likely internal candidates and you have to cover the succession with external, this highlights a potential risk in your succession management plans. It is good to ensure that your hires to senior roles are a healthy mix of promoted incumbents and external hires to bring new thinking but as always, its about getting the balance right. It is essential that career minded individuals within your business have some truth points and success stories from people that have made it to the top from within.

As part of the performance review process, where individuals are named on the succession plans, this should be discussed with them to check if this matches their aspiration for career progression and if it does what can be agreed as a development plan to help them get there.

As part of the succession management discussion with individuals it should always be pointed out that there are no guarantees of promotion or the ultimate timescales but this is about sharing a joint career development discussion to give encouragement, asses development needs and ensure every opportunity is made availiable for them to succeed. I have seen situations where good people have handed in their notice thinking that they would have to leave to gain promotion in another company, only to be told at that point that their line manager had always spoken very highly of them (to other people) and had identified them as a likely successor. A key point here is that you should let your good people know how valued they are and that they form part of your plans for the future of the business. This way your talented ambitious people will be much more likely to stick around for the long term.

6. **Exit Interviews** – If after all you efforts and hard work you still have people that want to leave, the exit interview is an ideal way to get feedback on what you can do better. People leave for all sorts of reasons some of which may be family related or nothing to do with their experience with you as an employer but it's vital that you find out. They say that good leadership is wanting to hear what you don't necessarily want to hear and the exit interview is the ideal time to get real honest feedback from an employee's perspective on why they have decided to leave. The tempting thing to do here is dismiss their reasons for leaving and put it down to the individual but all exit interview data should be collected and analysed to understand if there are any trends that can be reversed. In much the same way as you should design a consistent customer experience, you should also look for ways to improve the day to day experiences of your employees. Your aim should be that all leavers have good leaver status to protect your employer brand.

As we get to the end of chapter six you may be thinking that you have somehow been missold. You thought you were buying a book on strategy and you have just read a full chapter on what that reads like people management. The clue in the book's title is "wining", to win you have to take part and to take part and win you need the best players. Winning strategies do not implement themselves, engaged and talented employees who are clear what is expected of them and what the future holds are the the most important ingredient of any winning strategy.

7 The sales strategy

"You don't close a sale, you open a relationship if you want to build a long-term, successful enterprise.' Patricia Fripp

So you have the commanders intent from the CEO, grow sales by 10% year on year and arrive at £100M turnover in five years time without eroding profit margins. You have done a thorough discovery phase analysis of your product service offering and established your strategy around how you are going to position yourself and you have carefully designed the customer value proposition (i.e what makes your customers want what you are selling). You have aligned and engaged all of the people in your business and everyone is well and truly engaged. Now what you need is a sales strategy and I do not use the word strategy lightly. As with general business strategy there are many things to consider around a challenge to grow sales. There are also some common pitfalls to be avoided and I will start this section by describing an all too common but fundamentally flawed approach.

THE ABUNDANCE MENTALITY

Having received this year's sales target to achieve the plan, the Sales Director analyses the previous year's performance by each of her sales team and stretches their numbers. To demonstrate that some science has been applied she does not stretch them all by exactly 10% and she will give the more challenging targets to her overly ambitious sales people who are full of confidence in their own ability, encouraged by the promise of eye watering commission if they hit their numbers. There is no real assessment done to establish where exactly the increased sales will come from but each of her sales team know and have accepted that they need to do better than last year. When the Sales Director forecasts the sales over the next five years this will be through a combination of steady growth across all existing customers and new customers will be found to make up the extrapolated shortfall from the current customer base. The Sales Directors strategy is essentially to drive the sales team a little harder this year and progressively harder over the term of the 5 year plan. When looking at resources she may well have budgeted to include some new sales hires in the latter stages of the plan as the personal sales targets for her existing team would have been stretched to the edges of superhuman capability. The hypothesis of the abundance mentality is to assume that all of your customers will want increasingly more of what you have to offer and your salespeople will become increasingly more efficient and making sure they get it. If this abundance mentality sounds a little bit like your current sales plan, then you have my sympathy and a guarantee that this next section will be worth the read.

As with your main business strategy, the production of your sales strategy starts with a discovery phase and the best place to start is with the sales data you already have. Once you have completed the discovery phase you will be able to allocate the companies valuable sales resources to gain maximum value. All workable strategies must take cognisance of the fact that unlike the abundance mentality you have a finite amount of resources and generally so do your customers.

Planning Your Sales Revenue Profile

Dependent on which industry you operate in your sales revenue may be subject to seasonal fluctuations during the busier months as illustrated in the following charts.

TYPICAL UK CONSTRUCTION REVENUE PROFILE

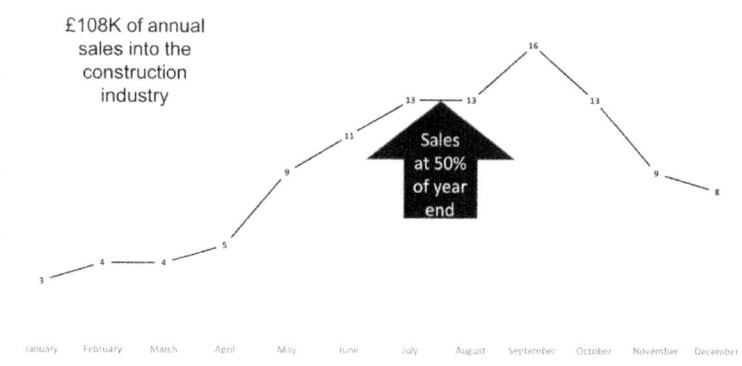

Figure 17 Construction revenue profile

The construction revenue profile builds to a peak over the summer months and also can experience dips over the Easter and Christmas holidays.

TYPICAL RETAIL REVENUE PROFILE

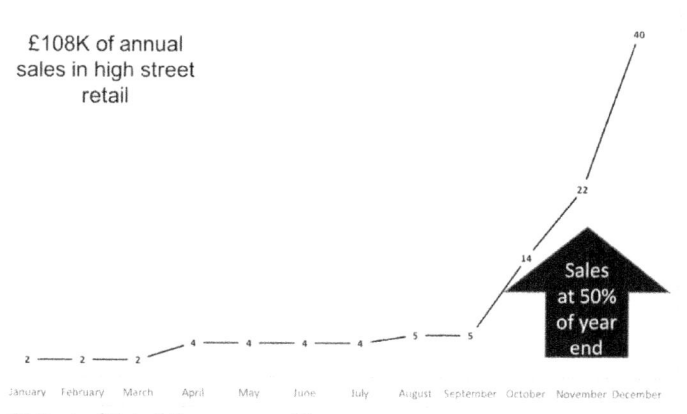

Figure 18 Typical Retail Revenue profile

The above chart shows a typical £108K revenue profile for a high street store where most of the annual sales are generated in the run up to the Christmas period.

LINEAR REVENUE PROFILE

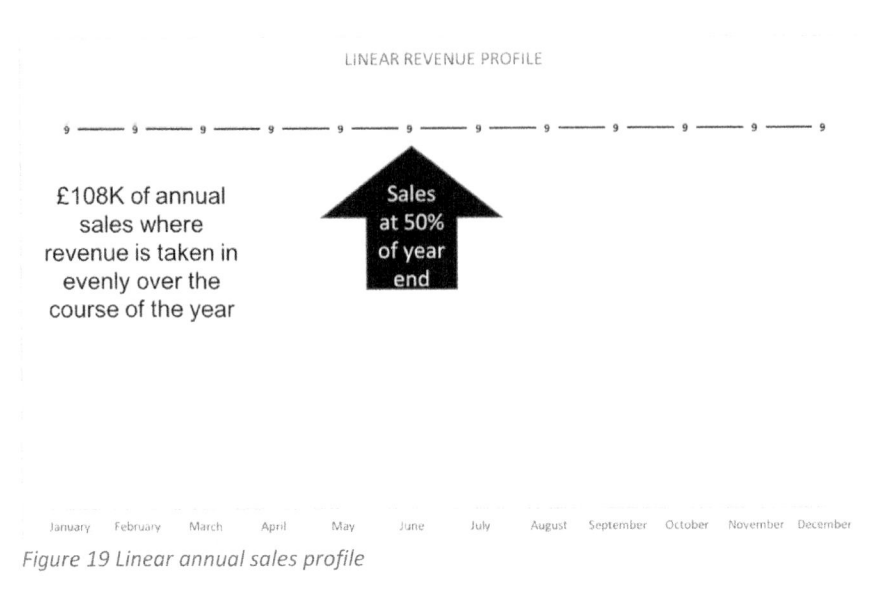

£108K of annual sales where revenue is taken in evenly over the course of the year

Sales at 50% of year end

January February March April May June July August September October November December

Figure 19 Linear annual sales profile

The above chart illustrates the same £108K revenue where the sales are achieved evenly over the course of the year. This could represent a convenience store or petrol station with no discernable seasonal differences.

The three examples have been given to illustrate that from a planning perspective the same £108K per year in sales could mean something very different both in terms of monthly sales expectations and peaks and troughs in business activity and resource requirements. Another consideration for your sales plan and forecasting is the length of time it takes to convert an order received into revenue. If your business is very transactional such as in retail there is little to no lag between order placement and the actual sale. In construction you may have a contractor that has a 3 month lead time between order receipt and doing the work to recognise the revenue. Understanding these timing differences for your own business is very important for target setting, resource planning and understanding what good looks like compared to your plan.

Below I have added an order intake profile onto the sales profile on the assumption there is a 3 month average lag from receipt of order to the generated sale which would be typical in construction.

ORDER INTAKE AND REVENUE PROFILE - CONSTRUCTION

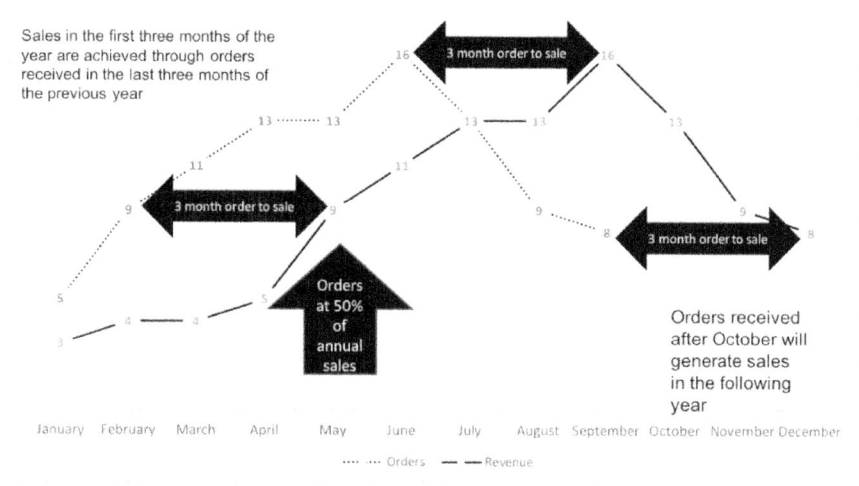

Figure 20 Order intake and revenue with a 3 month lag

Having an appreciation for the time lag is a very important aspect of the sales strategy. In the example above to generate £108K of revenue in the year you will need to have an order book of £108K by the end of September as any orders received after that date will be unlikely to be delivered and sold by year end. Therefore the targets and the timings for the sales team to receive orders in the above example needs to stay 3 months ahead of the targeted revenue profile. I appreciate the above may be a little complicated but it's an important point that I have seen overlooked on many occasions. In the worst cases the monthly order intake targets for the sales team are spread out evenly over the entire year. In this kind of situation you would end up with the sales team asking for a bonus as they hit their order intake targets by 31st December but the business essentially failing because it could not convert the orders to sales within the financial year. In order to understand what the order intake and revenue profile needs to look like for your own business, the best thing to do is use historical data and look for the pattern profile and the order intake lag (if indeed there is one).

Once you have your sales target and you understand what your order intake target needs to look like to achieve it, you now need to plan for where the orders are going to come from. Again the best place to start is your order book from the previous year especially if your business is based on a large proportion of repeat customers but of course this will also depend on what you are selling and what the replacement cycle is for the product or service. As an example if you were selling bed mattresses and it is recommended to change them every eight years, you would use your customer list of eight years ago to generate a sales call list for the current year. If on the other hand you would expect to deal with all your customers at least once a year, it is best to start with some fundamental questions from the previous years data as a starting point for this year's sales plan:-

1. **Customer base** – has the total number of customers increased or decreased over the last financial year? This can be an important metric especially if as part of your sales strategy you want to reduce your overall dependency on a few key customers where your Porter's Five Forces analysis had identified high customer power. Improving the quantity of customer mix helps to de-risk the business from being overly reliant on a few key accounts.

2. **New and non customers** – this is worth checking also as an overall rise in your number of customers may hide a significant shift in your customer base. For example you may look at the customer base growth from 2015 across 2016 and see that from a closing position in 2015 you had 3500 customers which grew to 3628 customers by the end of 2016. This however does not tell the full story that is needed for the sales strategy. The following illustration shows that during 2016 there was a reduction of 684 customers that you had done business with in 2015 but not in 2016. The overall increase in new customers in 2016 of 824 had masked the none customer number. The reduction of the 684 customers in 2016 may well have been based on no requirements for your product or service or it may have been as a result of drift to the competition. One of the key call lists for the sales team would be the none customers in 2016 to see if you could get them and their much valued revenue and profit back.

BUILDING A WINNING BUSINESS STRATEGY

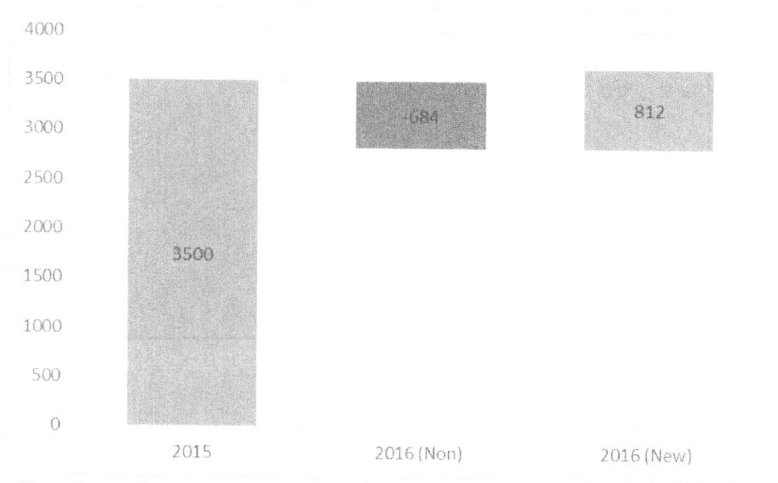

[Bar chart showing: 2015 = 3500; 2016 (Non) = 684; 2016 (New) = 812]

Figure 21 customer base movements for sales planning

3. **Average spend per customer** – This is another valuable metric that you can gain real insight from. The table below details the average spend by customers in 2015 and 2016.

Column1	2015	2016
No of Customers	3500	3628
Total Revenue	£63,000,000	£64,500,000
Ave. Sales per customer	£18,000	£17,778

Figure 22 Average sales per customer for 2015-16

Even though the total number of customers had increased and there has been a growth in overall sales revenue, the average sales per customer has reduced. This is only a small reduction in average sales per customer but if the trend continues it could lead to future problems in sales growth as increasingly more customers will have to be found to counteract the effect of the diminishing returns per customer. As we are only dealing in averages here and the difference is only small, there is an additional piece of analysis on the sales data that can be undertaken to give a more powerful view of your total sales performance and to give some helpful data on the production of the sales strategy. If you run a frequency distribution on the sales by customer for 2015 and 2016 and segment the customer numbers by their total spend per annum you can get a much more interesting view of the sales activity across the two years.

	2015	2016
Total Customers	3500	3628
>£500,000	5	6
£300,000 - £499,000	7	8
£100,000 - £299,000	24	25
£50,000 - £99,999	590	591
£25,000 - £49,999	548	568
£10,000 - £24,999	380	238
<£10,000	1,946	2,193

Figure 23 grouped spend by customers 2015-16

Having taken the time to do the additional analysis on the historical sales numbers, the above table now reveals some significant shifts in the customer spend activity that would have been missed if you had only looked at overall average sales per customer. The first observation is that the number of customers who had spent less than £10K in the year had increased from 1,946 in 2015 to 2,193 in 2016. This high number of low spend customers has been the reason for the decline in the average sales per customer. This may be because of the 812 new customers in 2016 and further analysis could be done to establish this. The encouraging thing from the table however is the increase in customers that are spending greater than £100,000/year. This overall number has increased from 36 in 2015 to 39 in 2016. Categorising the customers by how much they spend will help you to understand where your sales resources should be allocating their time to get the best results.

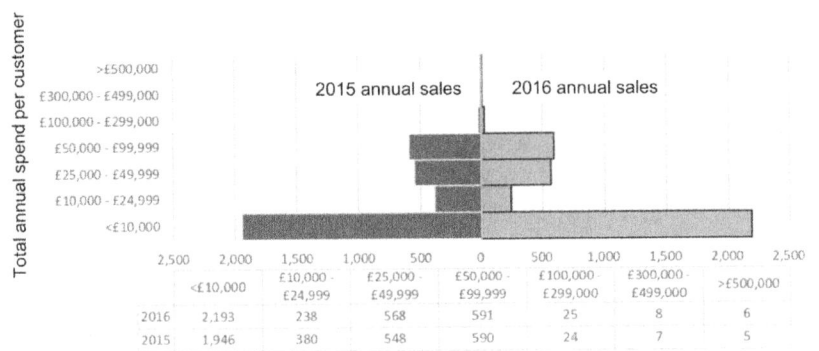

Figure 24 Segmented customer annual sales volumes

As well as keeping historical spend data on your customers it should also be part of your insights selling process to establish how much each of your customers have actually got to spend. Of course this depends what it is your selling. If its luxury goods like watches and handbags then your customers will always find the money if they want something badly enough but if you are selling advertising space business to business for example your customers will only have a finite budget for advertising. If your customer spends £300K a year with you and they have an advertising budget of £300K, this is a very different proposition than if they spend £300K a year with you but their budget is £1M. In this latter example it means that the account has potential to grow faster in the short term than the customers overall need as they are currently doing £700K of business with your competition. As part of developing your sales strategy, it is best to segment your customers into manageable groups by sales focus. This of course can be by product/service line, geography etc. but also it can be useful to segment your customer groups by their size and sales potential.

BRONZE TO PLATINUM SEGMENTATION

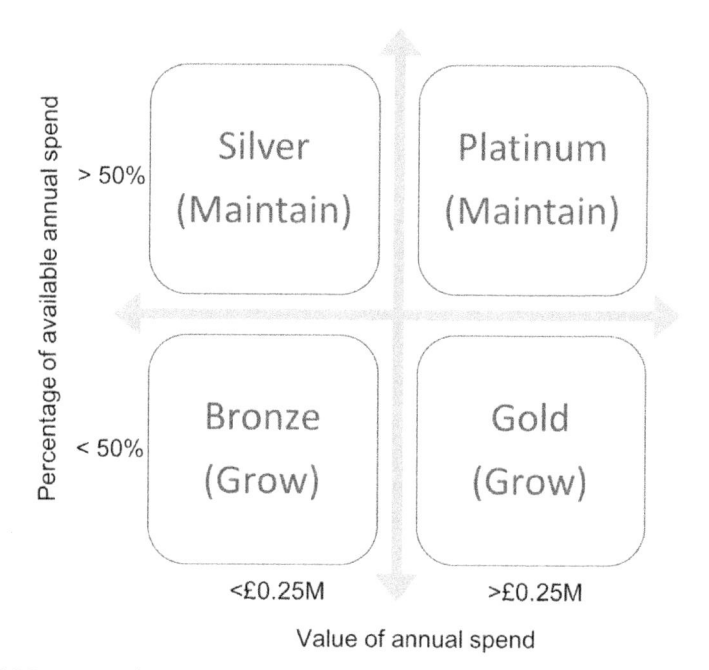

	<£0.25M	>£0.25M
> 50%	Silver (Maintain)	Platinum (Maintain)
< 50%	Bronze (Grow)	Gold (Grow)

Percentage of available annual spend / Value of annual spend

Figure 25 Bronze to platinum customer segmentation

The above simple four box grid illustration has two axes for percentage of customers annual spend and the total value of their annual spend. You simply have to adjust the value scale for your own business and you can set this as the median sales figure or whatever nominal value you consider would give you a meaningful segmentation for your own sales strategy going forward.

Bronze – These are customers who in the last 12 months have spent less than £250K and whom you believe give you less than half of their overall annual business in your product or service category. These may be new customers who are not yet fully confident in you or they may have a deliberate policy of using multiple suppliers to keep healthy competition on price and service. These are classed as grow accounts over the longer term. The significance of these bronze customers may not be business critical to today's overall sales but these may be fledgling companies that you can develop a long term lasting relationship with and grow as they grow. The bronze customers may also collectively form a significant proportion of your overall customer base which will need to be actively managed and protected from the competition.

Silver – These are customers who in the last 12 months have spent less than £250K and whom you believe give you more than half of their overall annual business. There is of course a large potential difference in monetary terms between 60% and 90% of their business so it's a judgement call in terms of your growth aspirations with the silver customer group. These customers need to be actively maintained which is a very different proposition from being ignored. You need to establish and agree the right level of customer support whilst not damaging the relationship through over selling, after all with over 50% of their spend on your product it's a mathematical fact that you are already their favorite supplier of what you have to sell. The trick with the maintain accounts is to keep it that way.

Gold – These are customers who in the last 12 months have spent more than £250K and whom you believe give you less than half of their overall annual business in your product or service category. These gold customers are ideal targets to support business growth as they have the potential to have a material impact on your sales fortunes in the short to medium term. With a finite level of sales resource in the organisation I would recommend the gold customer group as your biggest source of additional sales potential. They are existing customers who are familiar with your product and at these sales levels you will have advocates of your business on the customers side of the fence. The sales activity should centre around what your company will need to do to grow these into a platinum customers where you secure the majority of their wallet share.

Platinum – These are customers who in the last 12 months have spent more than £250K and whom you believe give you more than half of their overall annual business. These are **must keep** customers as any losses of Platinum customers will have a significant material impact on your short to medium term sales. Their loyalty must not be taken for granted, so a little like the Silver customers, these are maintain accounts so it's about getting the levels of support and contact just right to prevent them being tempted away by the competition.

The bronze to platinum grid is very useful for segmentation of customers but the approach comes with a few words of caution. Firstly this categorisation of customers into precious metals is for internal consumption only and is used to determine strategy and the use of the companies resources to sell and maintain the relationships with each group. **I hope it goes without saying that as far as your customers are concerned they are all platinum and get the same level of service**. The grid and its completion only represents a specific moment in time and if compiled as I described above, the positions will have been derived from the previous year's sales data. The important thing to be mindful of when using this grid, is where are the customers now and where are they heading in the future. I will use the product lifecycle chart that I used in the earlier section to illustrate the point but in much the same way that your business may have a finite lifecycle, so might your customers. It's tempting to believe that your best customers will always be around to spend money with you but this is more likely to be constantly evolving. As part of your sales strategy, as well as gathering spend data and wallet share on your customers, you should also understand which customers will offer you a greater bang for your buck in terms of where you spend your time and effort on long term strategic relationships. In 1998 Google would have been someone's bronze customer and Enron would have been someone's Platinum customer. When assessing your customer base, you should make sure you do not over expose yourself financicially to a customer that is obviously struggling but also make sure you have a working knowledge of your customer base and study form in terms of whether they are growing or shrinking, what are the market conditions in which they trade and what if any are their seasonal buying cycles.

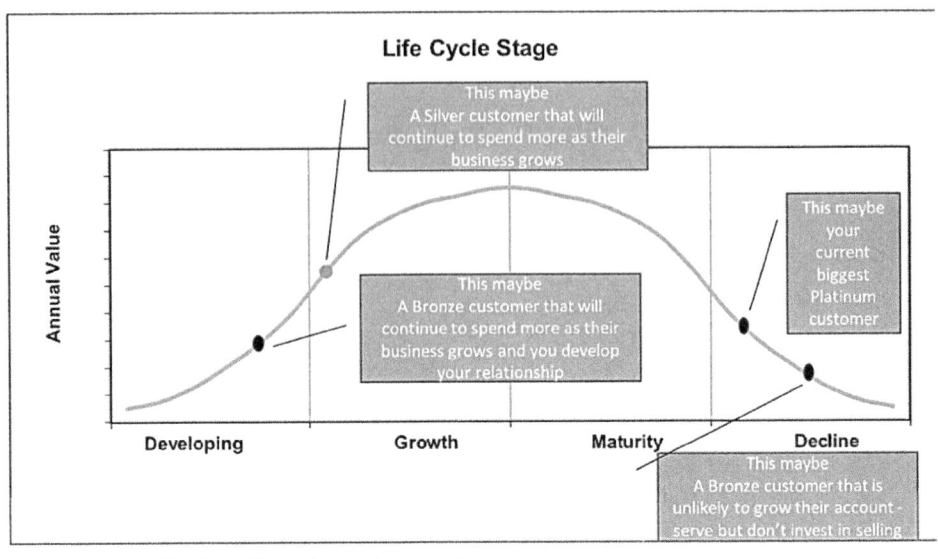

Figure 26 Customer business lifecycles and account status

Another consideration for where to invest your sales resource is market sectors. As well as understanding where a customer sits along the lifecycle, it is also to important to understand about the various market sectors that you are serving. As an example if you supply house bricks, then your product will be limited to the construction sector and a recessionary downturn in construction would have a major impact on your sales. If however you were in the stationery business you would be less likely to be impacted by a downturn in construction as you would have a customer base that would span multiple sectors. That is of course unless you are unlucky enough to work for construction stationary supplies limited. As previously mentioned understanding any seasonal as well as sector sensitivity can help with your sales strategy. As an example I used to run a business that hired generator floodlights into the rail industry but the hires were predominantly over the winter when the engineering workload was heaviest and Monday to Friday in overnight engineering works possessions. To improve the utilisation of the assets we started to hire the floodlights into the events industry at weekends over the summer. This meant changing the focus of our sales activity to improve the return on investment of the equipment but this was deliberate targeted strategy that took full cognisance of the seasonal cycles of the customer base.

Figure 27 With these blue chip customers, what could possibly go wrong?

CUSTOMER WIN BACK STRATEGY

You cannot hit a target you cannot see so please be careful not to forget the ones that got away. If we take the earlier example where we looked at customer movements between 2015 and 2016, we had in fact lost 684 customers over the trading year (Figure 21). These customers will not appear on any of your customer segment analysis as their details will be missing from the 2016 supplier accounts. So often when businesses lose customers, they don't take the time to understand why. Often the salesperson will blame the customer and will not spend sufficient time and or energy in understanding what if anything went wrong with a view to winning them back. In the UK we are not very good at complaining, so if an element of a product or service is not to our liking we will often say nothing and vote with our feet or increasingly with the click of a mouse. A good example of an industry that understands the benefit of customer retention is the TV/Broadband providers. They have the advantage of having to be informed when we intend to cancel our subscription and then we will promptly be put through to the account retention team who will give us faster broadband, more channels etc. just to keep our business. They do this because it is significantly more costly to attract a new customer than it is to keep an existing one. As an example in most companies 100% of the marketing budget is aimed at new customers as the existing ones do not need to be marketed to. The chart below illustrates what should be paid attention to in terms of efficiency and effectiveness be your top three sales priorities.

Chances of additional sales success

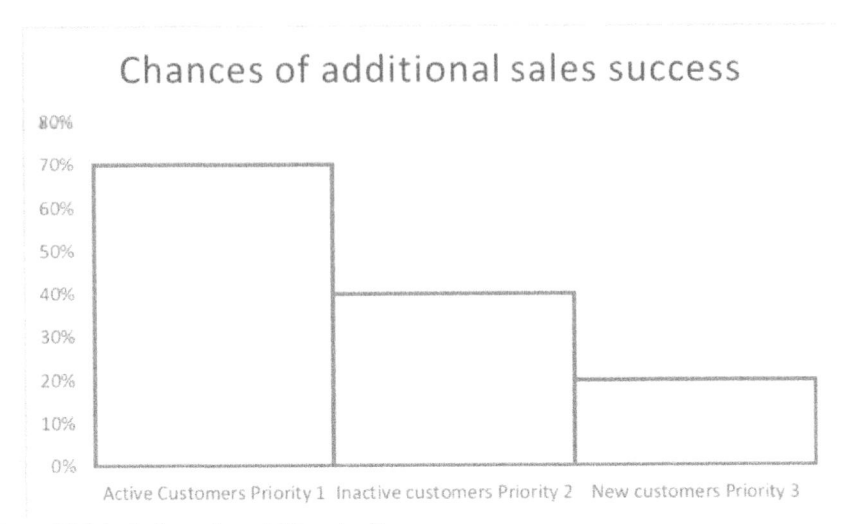

Figure 28 Priority focus for additional selling

So in pursuit of the CEO's goal of £100M sales, the best place to start is with your existing customer base as the average customer is 60-70% more likely to buy from you on the basis that they are familiar with your product and they are already using you. Your approach could be to sell more of the same to this customer at improved rates and service or upsell alternative offerings into your existing relationship. (wallet share expansion sales strategy)

The next priority should be your none or inactive customer list as these are between 20-40% more likely to use you again for a given amount of marketing activity. They are already familiar with your product but you have to understand and overcome whatever issues are present that turned them into a none customer in the first place. This may not always be about offering freebies or credits, it may just be a simple case of lower than average service left your customer with a bitter taste in their mouth. They did the very British thing of saying nothing but took their business elsewhere half expecting you to be on the phone within two weeks trying to find out what the problem was. This is an all too common scenario and problems are compounded if 18 months passes and a new salesperson on the patch tries to win back old customers. By now your once loyal customer has switched allegiance to your competitor who have served them very well over the last 18 months while you seamingly ignored them. Newly lost customers are like freshly baked bread and you have a window of opportunity over the following few days ideally to win them back, the quicker you act to get them back the better. Newly baked bread does not get better with age and the longer you leave it the harder it gets. Conducting a customer service questionaire at the end of each piece of activity is a great way of establishing confidence in whether that particular customer will use you again. If the feedback is not that flattering, do not get annoyed, get on the phone and do anything you can to win them back. Of the 682 lost customers if up to 40% of these can be won back this should be a priority for your sales team. Instead because we don't like rejection or fear conflict we make up imaginary tales to comfort ourselves and go hunting for new customers where it feels like the excitement of the chase and going out dating all over again. The problem is that new customers will only respond to between 5-20% of our sales overtures for a given piece of marketing activity but this is where salespeople seem to spend the second largest proportion of their time after existing customers. Remember your inactive customers will either come back to you or provide you with valuable feedback on what it is that has made their return unlikely, either way this is a good investment in sales time to ensure customer retention going forward is less of an issue. You should always try and absolutely minimise poor customer feedback through the service you deliver but when your service has been genuinely terrible and every company gets it wrong sometimes, it's how you respond to your customers complaints that can make all the difference. Sometimes lifelong customers can be created after snatching victory from the jaws of defeat and turning a disaster into a pleasant and surprising solution. If on the other hand you have been that terrible there is no way back, then listening to the feedback will be uncomfortable but all learning happens on the edge of comfort zones. The very worst feedback is your most valuable free consultancy and what you should do is learn from it because you might think that your customer is wrong but their perception in this case is very much your reality.

Setting Selling Objectives

Having looked at some of the supporting data on which you can build your plan you are now in a position to set some tangible S.M.A.R.T objectives for each of your sales team. I was once talking with the CEO of an Australian plant hire business and he told me that he only gave his salespeople two objectives a year. 1) Make a minimum of 10 sales calls a week 2) Do $1 Million in sales a year. I responded by saying that I thought he had given his salespeople at least one objective too many and the reason I gave for this statement was that an objective around the sales calls had insufficient substance and detail to elicit the desired sales performance. At the end of the year what would you do with a salesperson who has made an average of 18 sales calls a week but had only achieved $800,000 in sales?

In the following chart I have listed a set of objectives for Salesperson A and Salesperson B which if completed successfully would achieve the same in year headline sales performance but with very different outcomes for the longer term success of the organisation.

Salesperson A	Salesperson B
Achieve annual sales of £1.2M (100% Bonus)	Achieve annual sales of £1.2M (120% Bonus)
	Deductions for none achievement of the following:-
	At least £200k from Bronze customers (-10%)
	At least £500k from Silver customers (-5%)
	At least £300k from Gold customers (-10%)
	At least £300k from Platinum customers (-5%)
	Less than 15% customer attrition from previous year (-10%)
	At least 30 first time new customers > £20K spend (-10%)

Salesperson A – The single objective for this salesperson has the advantage of clarity but what it gains in clarity it loses in unintended negative consequences. This objective may seem a little too simple but I have seen much worse than this in the past where sales objectives have not even included financial targets. The key incentive for the salesperson here is all about the invoiced sales number and takes no cognisance of how each customer segment needs to cultivated for the longer term success of the business. If the customer has a dispute and tries to resolve it with the salesperson, there is no incentive for the salesperson to settle the dispute amicably by offering a credit against an invoice and consequently impacting their sales bonus for the year. There are also no incentives for the pursuit of new customers which generally take more effort to get traction as I described earlier in this section. Without the specific incentives around new customers the salesperson would likely take the path of least resistance and deal with a narrow cross section of the existing customer base to achieve the target.

Salesperson B - This set of objectives is designed to not only achieve the desired overall sales level, but to offer incentive and disincentives to guide a broader range of focus from the salesperson. You could argue that if this salesperson achieves all of their objectives then this will cost the business 20% more in sales bonus but I would argue that this is a premium worth paying for. I will explain the rationale and the psychology behind the structured deductions from the bonus later in the book.

As a final note on the sales targets, I would always advise that the sum total of the sales targets across your sales team as a minimum add up to the overall required sales target for the business. Ideally targets should overshoot your required sales number so that if all sales targets were achieved then this would result in an outperformance for the year. When setting sales targets where the sum of the parts is greater than the whole, there are two things that should be considered.

1. **Anticipate and plan for success** – sales targets should be challenging but achievable. If all of your sales team do achieve their targets and this results in an over performance equating to 130% of your targeted sales figure, then you need to make sure that your operational delivery of the stretched target does not let the customer down by putting too much strain on the business. In order to make sure the business is ready for and can anticipate increased demand, regular updates on performance and the resulting resource requirements need to be articulated and clearly understood by all. A common pitfall that arises from the healthy tension that can exist between sales and operations is that sales do not give enough notice to the operational teams and the operational teams start to struggle with delivery, which it turn impacts the customer which makes life harder for the salesperson. This vicious circle spirals until the operations and sales teams are so busy battling each other that they forget about the customer and of course the customer pretty soon forgets about you.

2. **Have an open book policy on budgets and sales targets** – of course by this I do not mean with everybody but you need to be absolutely straight with the sales team in terms of what the overall sales target is, what the sum of the parts adds up to and the overall contingency in the sales plan. As an example you could have an annual sales target of £30M but the individual team sales targets add up to £32M giving a £2M contingency. It is not uncommon for some people to council that we tell the sales team that there is no contingency and that £32M is the sales target for the business. Their rationale for such tactics is that they are concerned that the sales team will perform better if they think there is no contingency. This is a flawed argument as each individual sales person should be incentivised to achieve their own targets but much more important than this, it's all about trust and attempts to be disingenuous around targets can quickly destroy teamwork which can be a long and uncomfortable journey back if not handled correctly.

Understanding the Customer and Buyer Personas

As well as identifying your target customers and understanding what you would like from them by way of business, it is also worthwhile to create a set of buyer personas so you can tailor your sales approach accordingly. How you present your product and service will very much depend on the needs of the buyer or specifically the individual that will be responsible for placing the order. Your product or service may be exactly the same in each case but you may package it with slightly different messages dependent on the buying persona in your customers organisation. In a very small business you may be dealing with the owner manager but the same offer into a large organisation may be handled by buyers with slightly different wants and needs from the relationship.

CEO/Supply Chain Director – keep the pitch at a high level spelling out the benefits of your company and how you are a close fit to their sustainability and supply chain strategy. They will be interested in value for money, a sound financial pedigree and overall ease of doing business with a single point of contact and clarity around terms and conditions. Demonstrating that you will do what you are saying you are going to do.

Local estates manager – you have an opportunity to present your case from the estates managers perspective and potentially include an element of free consultancy so that he will champion your product and in the process make himself look good for his leadership teams.

Graduate Buyer – do not send paper based media to sell the product, have a full social platform and build the relationship online together with a self-service portal full of media and supporting information. This is about building a long term relationship and making sure that this buyer in their early years in industry gets familiar and confident about what you have to offer.

The buyers persona should always be an important part of your pitch consideration but at the most basic level, this is about putting yourself in your customers shoes and making sure that you clearly articiulate the benefits of what you are selling and in a way that resonates with your audience. As a customer what are the service levels they can expect as a minimum.

Winning Tenders

If as part of your companies selling process you have to respond to invitations to tender I have detailed below a few hints and tips that may just improve your conversion rate. First of all though you must consider all invitations to tender against your strategic choices for the business (Figure 15 page 35). Each time you agree to and respond to an invitation to tender, you are committing in the first instance to invest time and resources to secure future work for your organisation. Remember strategy is all about the choices you make and sometimes this purely comes down to what you are willing to say yes or no to as a business. If you have taken the time to complete the strategic choices grid for your business, this should be used as the yardstick for all you go/no go tender decisions. Another reason why strategies fail is that companies do not hold true to their strategic choices when they run into problems with order intake and decide to start tendering the wrong types of work for the wrong types of reasons. Each time a new Invitation To Tender (ITT) is received, this must be assessed against the true strategic choices and criteria for the business. If the company strategy is to change its course in the type of work it undertakes, there will inevitably be a period of time following the strategic launch when you receive ITT's that are more closley aligned to you old business strategy and you must resist all temptation to price for work that does not fit the new strategy. As I referenced earlier, when compiling a business strategy you have to have in mind how this will be sold and communicated to the rest of the business. Maybe the first time your strategy will be truly pressure tested after the launch is when you have received an ITT that specifically matches the type of work that your strategy had espoused you move away from. This is the perfect opportunity to send a clear message on the new strategic direction of the company, which in the early days of the new strategy will require a considerable amount of courage and conviction in the senior team to hold the line on message discipline and message consistency. Assuming however that the ITT does match your chosen stratregic customer profile and work type and you have decided to return a tender, then the tips below should help improve you chances of winning:-

1. **Answer the exam question** – if your tender is going to be opened by a panel make sure that you make it as easy as possible for them to interpret your bid. It is usually a good idea to copy the scope of works/service provision and play it back to them in your tender return, with a statement that clearly says included against each element. You want to get the panel on your side so doing everything you can to make it easy for them

to interpret your price and offering will go a long way.
2. **Use their own language** – go on the customers website, look at their values, get an understanding of their vision, mission statement and their terminology. Play their own terminology back to them for example if they talk about their ambition to have zero waste to landfall by 2020 as part of their sustainability policy. You might want to add additional wording into your product or service description that demostrates how your company would help them achieve zero waste to landfill.
3. **If you are selling a service introduce the team** – people buy from people they like. A smiling photograph of each of your team with a short bio is a great way to draw a prospective customer closer to you. If you look at a picture of a smiling face you smile back. In his brilliant Book "Influence", Dr Robert Chialdini places likability in his top six scientifically proven powers of influence.
4. **Gain credibility** – as well as having an attractive price and introducing your people, you will need to convince the customer that you are the right people for the job. Include case studies of similar work and provide references to support your submission. If you have people on your team with expert technical qualifications then include these, it promotes peace of mind and authority power to your submission.
5. **Gain Trust** – if you do have a weakness in your tender do not try to gloss over it, ignore it or hide it. If you have a weakness in your submission bring it to the customers attention early in your bid documents and then describe how you will overcome this perceived weakness. Another one of Chialdini's top 6 powers of influence is trust and bringing out your own weakneses before the customer spots them is a great way to get them onside. All too often companies try and throw you off the scent of their biggest weakness and generally leave it up to you to find out. When a weakness is found out by the client, no amount of trying to recover the situation will gain you any trust. I was once in a presentation to a customer for a multimillion pound factory modification and at that time we were punching a little above our weight but we wanted desperately to get on their tender list for the project. Before the client had an opportunity to raise any concerns over our size and capability to take on such a large project I told them that if we were successful on the project this would be the largest project that we would have ever done and as such we would dedicate our best team to the project to

ensure its success. Immediately this took the wind out of the clients sails and the Chief Engineer from their side lent forward and said that this was the biggest project they they had ever done also. We were subsequently placed on the tender list and the feedback from the presentation majored on the fact that we had been totally honest and open and had not tried to hide our inexperience. Both sides opening up in this way had already inadvertantly started the team building process necessary to deliver the job.

We ultimately lost the job on price but therein lies another valuable lesson. Using persuasion and influence techniques in bid situations can only get you so far if your price is not right. If your price is right however, it will help to reinforce the buying decision and in bid situations you need to use all the tools at your disposal to improve your conversion rate.

6. **Go large on the deliverables** – show the customer just how much you value their potential custom by the quality of your submission. Your tender return may be the first time you have submitted anything to this prospective customer and you only get one chance to make a first impression. Make your submission feel like the quality and presentation that you want your company to be famous for. Sending back a one page piece of paper with the price on it could be considered as answering the exam question but it speaks volumes about your organisation and the quality of the service the client may get if they were to take you up on your offer. The mantra I believe holds true, the customer will quite literally weight your tender return, on the weight of your tender return.

8 Scenario Planning

"The problem with the future is that it is different. If you are unable to think differently, the future will always arrive as a surprise." Gary Hamel"

So by now you have reached a point in the process where the discovery phase has been completed, the strategic choices have been made, a strategy map has been created and you have a sense of the business areas that need to be addressed to support your business growth. An overall sales target has been established with segments across the customer groups and you have an understanding of how your sales need to be incentivised across the sales team.

We have now arrived at what for some would be the starting point of the strategic process. This is the point at which financial scenario modeling will help shape the feasibility of achieving the CEO's lofty sales targets. A very common mistake at this point is to dive for the excel spreadsheets and manipulate and stretch until you arrive at a sales glide path that somehow like a moth to a flame achieves a £100M sales figure in the final year of the 5 year plan. This saves a lot of time as you already know that the answer is £100M and anything less than that might make you look bad and the CEO could accuse you of not being ambitious enough or failing to think outside the preverbial box. You produce a 5 year sales profile that gets increasingly ambitious from year 3 onwards so you don't put too much pressure on yourselves in years 1 and 2. The graphs looks good, all the numbers add up and you devise a strategic commentary that explains away the fact that our future performance in terms of both sales and profitability will be a lot better than it ever has been in the past when all of our current problems are out of the way. If this is a scenario that sounds familiar do not despair, it is all too common. The numbers add up, the larger elements of the sales growth are back end loaded and a lot can happen over the next few years. The problem is that this approach was used just over 2 years ago and now halfway through the term of the previous plan, there is a general acceptance that the old strategy is no longer achievable and so what was sold as a strategic review to get the business back on track has turned into more empty promises of "jam tomorrow".

This is where your strategic plan needs to be grounded in reality. The problem with the scenario modelling is that we tend to have positive confirmation bias and constantly look for evidence to support the achievement of our target. I'm not suggesting this is done maliciously it is merely a fact that our positive bias needs to be kept in check and a good starting point for this is to dust off the previous 5 year plan and read the commentary and assumptions that were made. The chances are that the plan will read very well and as you go through the assumptions and supportive commentary it may sound pretty much like the ones you had lined up for this latest new and improved version of the strategy. The problem is as Warren Buffet (Chairman of Berkshire Hathaway) said "in the business world, the rearview mirror is always clearer than the windshield".

So as you review the previous strategy you will notice that it is not full of outlandish and near impossible feats of engineering and customer excellence and in fact the strategic commentary very much made sense in terms of what needed to be done to grow the customer base, so why did it not happen? There are two fundamental reasons for this and the first as briefly mentioned is the confirmation bias and the inclusion of a whole host of opportunities that are not a work of fiction but are not sufficiently countered by potential downside and challenges that are inevitable in every business. The second reason is the lack of time and attention that was given to the execution of the strategy and the action plans needed to deliver it. When we make plans in business we tend to under estimate the amount of time things take by about 50%, especially when they are running alongside what we call the day job. As part of the scenario planning process you should be mindful about fine tuning the parameters and assumptions of the strategy and looking at a range of potential outcomes. I have listed below a few of the key challenges to consider as part of the planning process:-

1. **Take a look at the recent past** – Is there reason to believe from the recent performance that your projections are achievable. If you have only ever been a 4% operating profit company are you really comfortable that you have sufficient confidence from the actions in your plan to make you a 10% profit company going forward. Einstein said "the definition of insanity is doing the same thing over and over again and expecting different results". What is going to change and bridge the gap between the performance of the recent past and the near future targets that you have in your new business plan.

2. **Opportunities are usually disguised as hard work** – as part of the strategic planning process, you may have built up your strategy map and looked at ways you can upskill your people, ways that you can improve the systems and processes, add more

value for the customers, take cost out of the supply chain. The problem here is the shear amount of resource required to do anything other than the day job. Strategic opportunities are important but are generally not urgent as by their very nature the benefit is realised in the future rather than here and now, as a consequence the potential opportunities will often be the first items in the diary to get moved when a fire needs putting out.

3. **We are not good with delayed gratification** – delivering strategy is all about delayed gratification and we live in a world with short feedback loops where we want to go home each night feeling like we have accomplished something. Strategy is about the long game but in business we monitor progress daily, weekly and monthly. If the results seem too far off into the future we get fed up, lose enthusiasm and revert back to the day job if swift results from our strategic actions are not forthcoming. You need to be prepared to make time and resource investments today to deliver perfomance outside of the current financial year. As a leader, one of the hardest challenges is to instill balance between today's pressing problems and working on the strategy and we will spend an appropriate amount of time on this ourselves later in the book.

4. **The traffic lights are never all green on the way to work** – In an earlier section I said that strategy was analogous to a journey not a destination and yet if each identified opportunity was the equivalent to a green traffic light, we often convince ourselves that there is a steady stream of green traffic lights over the term of the plan with flawless timely delivery to achieve our goals. Your plans should be challenging but realistic and they should make allowances for the bumps in the road, even if at the time of planning you have not identified any, you need to have what I would call a healthy state of paranoia and a coordinated plan about things that may go wrong.

This is the point in the process to remove the rose tinted spectacles and get ruthless with your assessment of the chances of success. This piece of work will be very much a subjective judgement that you and your team should compile and as part of the strategic plan, it will give you a chance to articulate the things that can go wrong and what would need to be done to mitigate the risks and achieve success. As an example if you have a strategy aimed at increasing customer wallet share your competitors may respond with a price cut to retain the customer and so you would have to either forgo the additional business or secure it at a lower margin than your current run rate. There is a danger that you can get into paralysis by analysis and this is not an exact science but I like to use three simple mindsets in the scenario planning process.

Pessimistic (Glass half empty) – We all know at least one person in our team who's time it is to shine when looking for a pessimistic view, but this is a very healthy approach. Good strategic leadership is about having a healthy balance of enthusiasm and vision but this needs to be kept in check by the team pessimist. Often the team pessimist will offer up lessons learned and examples from the past that you would be foolish to ignore. This approach assumes that all the traffic lights will be at red and is a realisation of at least one or two major risks in our assumptions will at some point materialise. Taking a relatively dim view of the delivery of the strategy will at least give you a bottom range of expectation and will allow you to cut your resourcing and investment cloth accordingly. The thing to remember about pessimists, is that they can always point to the times that they were right.

Realistic – a prudent balanced view of the likelihood of achieving some but not all of the strategic objectives. This scenario will be probably the closest to the recent past performance or business as usual if there is such a thing and may model the current trend in growth and success with some modest adjustment for known investments and initiatives. This financial projection would be the one closest to what you expect the actual budgets and targets to be based on. Where a problem occurs with the realistic projections is that these are generally at odds with the CEO's world view which are generally towards the more optimistic end of the spectrum. This is not taking anything away from the CEO as it is their job to lead the team to results better than they thought they were capable of. There needs to be some healthy tension in the target setting so the business can keep moving forward and delivering the strategy.

Optimistic (Glass half full and it's rose tinted) - this scenario is about the art of the possible. This is another very healthy world view of what the future would look like as it will bring to the forefront considerations of rapid growth, talent, resources, systems and processes that would need to be in place. There are of course considerable risks associated with over trading which can be every bit as damaging if not more so than a downturn in activity. This scenario is all about out performance and what is the maximum possible expectation out of the strategic activity. This may be the scenario that the CEO wants you to deliver, but having done the exercise you will have considered the necessary investment in resources needed to achieve this performance level. I once recall having a conversation with my old CEO who was pushing me at the time in signing off on our small plant hire targets for the year. The previous year we had done £24M in hire revenue with good levels of utilisation and the CEO was trying to get me to sign up to delivering £29M in the following year. He also wanted me to do it without any capital investment in new equipment. As part of the discussion I stated that without any more equipment, I would have to increase my hire rate prices on average by 21% and still achieve the same levels of utilisation in a very cost focused construction hire market. He just smiled and said he had every confidence in me. As flattered as I was he still didn't get his £29M.

If you take your realistic sales profile as your baseline assumptions for expected growth over the term of the plan, then this should be properly pressure tested by as many as your team as possible to ensure there is sufficient robustness and challenge. Through this process of constructive dialogue you will arrive at a consensus which is a crucial milestone of gaining buy in that I will come onto in the next section. Once you and your team are happy with the baseline realistic sales profile, it is now time to look at identified risks and opportunities. Risks and opportunities by definition are things that may or may not happen, as an example see the following illustration.

BUILDING A WINNING BUSINESS STRATEGY

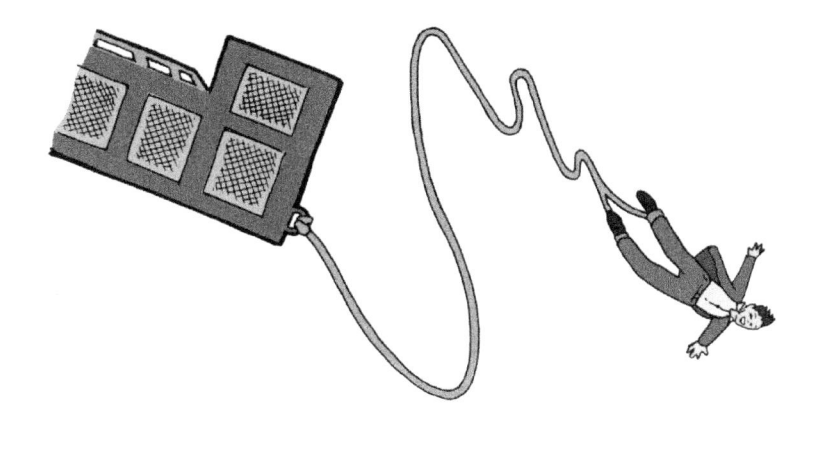

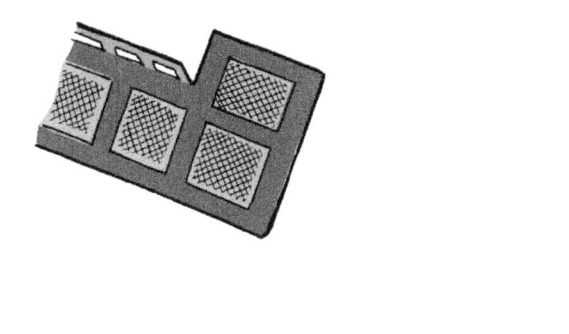

Figure 29 Some Risk and Zero Risk!

Bungee jumping is risky as it carries with it the possibility that something may go wrong and you could get seriously hurt. However bungee jumping without a bungee is not risky as there is an uncomfortable certainty as to what the outcome would be. A risk is something that may or may not happen and it should sit outside of your realistic financial assumptions. Likewise an opportunity is just that, until it actually happens it should also sit outside of your realistic financial model. What tends to happen in the strategic planning process is that we factor in the realisation of opportunities without fully taking account of the hard work and resources they will take to deliver.

The creation of a risk and opportunities register will serve a number of very useful purposes, in considering the bandwidth of the potential outcomes and what it will take to mitigate or avoid the risks and deliver the opportunities, this helps with resource planning and how the team need to focus their attention. If large risks can be significantly reduced for relatively little resource expenditure, then this would become a priority action during the execution phase.

The creation of a register in this way will also identify the full resource requirements and the support needed from the CEO if you want to achieve the outperformance number, some consideration for inclusion in the register would be :-

1. **Description of the risk or opportunity.**
2. **Ratings for impact** (1-4 usually a monetary scale from minor to major dependent on the financial strength of the business).
3. **Ratings for likelihood** (1-4 1-Unlikley to 4 very likely).
4. **Resultant risk score** (Impact * Likelihood) so a total risk score of 16 would demand a higher priority than a total risk score of 9 etc.
5. **Action required for best business outcome.**
6. **Risk / Opportunity Owner** (must be one individual).
7. **Resources required** to achieve desired outcome.
8. **Post treatment scores** for impact and likelihood (this checks if it is expected that the control measures will be adequate enough to either deliver the opportunity or reduce the risk to acceptable levels.
9. **By when -** some opportunities and risks are time bound such as dealing with the millennium bug, Brexit deadlines and others will be constant and ongoing.
10. **Potential financial impact** negative (risk) or positive (opportunity).

Once the risk and opportunities register has been completed if you total up the potential impact of all the risks and take this away from your realistic sales profile this will produce the pessimistic sales profile. Next total up all the positive upside from the opportunities and add this to the realistic profile to create the optimistic sales profile. In reality of course it will be unlikely that you would deliver such a polarised outcome one way or the other and most likely you will have a combination of ups and downs as the strategy unfolds and the competition and market reacts to it. This exercise is very useful as it effectively produces an expected upper and lower limit

BUILDING A WINNING BUSINESS STRATEGY

bandwidth of potential outcomes that will make it easier for resource planning aswell as managing expectations throughout the organisation.

Scenario Forecast in £M

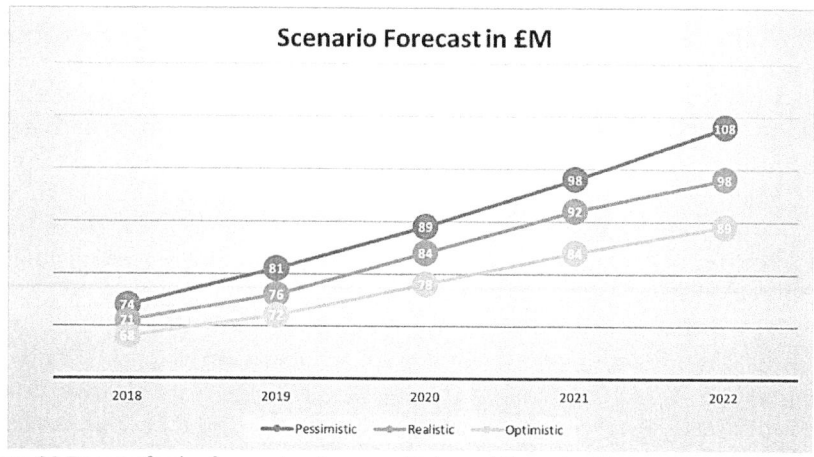

[Chart showing three scenario lines from 2018 to 2022:
- Pessimistic: 71, 72, 78, 84, 89
- Realistic: 74, 81, 89, 92, 98 (dark line with 84, 98 visible)
- Optimistic: 74, 81, 89, 98, 108]

Figure 30 Range of sales forecast outcomes - Risks and Opportunities

Once the risk register is completed this should be used as a live document where new risks and opportunities are added and outcomes are constantly reviewed and adjusted accordingly. If you imagine the three lines on the scenario chart as a large zip fastener, as time goes by as you update the risk register you may have had a risk valued at -£1M which materialises but actually impacts at -£840K. The register would be updated with the actual figure and lines for the realistic and pessimistic scenario will start to converge as you move through the plan. The chart below shows a conceptual scenario forecast at two years into the plan.

Scenario Forecast in £M

[Chart with Date Baseline showing Past actuals (2018-2019) converging and Future Scenario (2020-2022) diverging into three lines:
- 2018: 71; 2019: 89, 90, 91; 2020: 89, 93; 2021: 84, 92, 101; 2022: 89, 98, 110]

New opportunities and risks are constantly added and dealt with

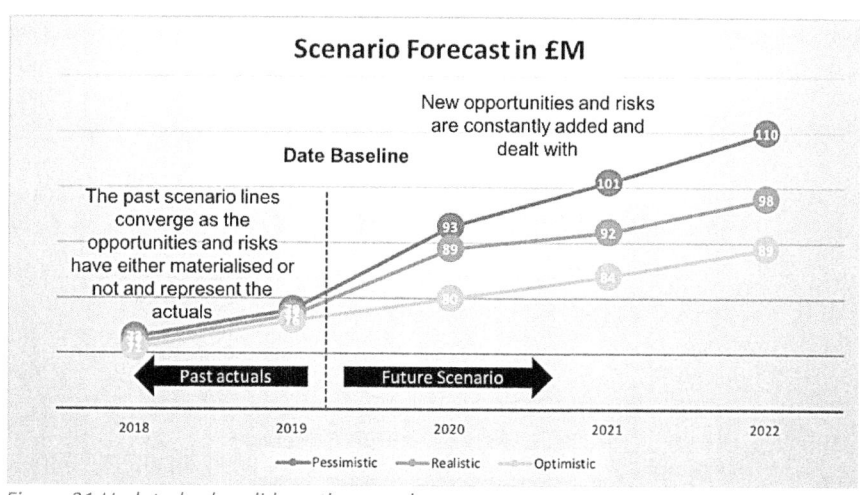

The past scenario lines converge as the opportunities and risks have either materialised or not and represent the actuals

Figure 31 Updated sales glide path example

As well as producing scenarios for sales, the same concept can be used for profit margins and it is best to produce a separate profile for profit as often an increase in sales volumes can be achieved through lower profit margins. It is worth remembering the euristic that in business revenue is vanity and profit is sanity. A relentless pursuit of sales without protecting the profit margin and of course cash can quickly turn you and your business into busy fools. All business is about risk and reward and every company has a core capability to manage and control a certain level of risk. Using a risk register to constantly monitor and adjust the companies risk profile can help with business decisions and keep your business out of trouble. If a business decision presents either an opportunity or a risk, it is worth considering if the risk is worth it. For example you may have an opportunity to get involved in the tender for a large supermarket project which would represent the largest single opportunity that your company had been involved in and give you a high profile project to put your business on the map. You learn that taking this project on would carry significant risks associated with its timely completion as the damages associated with a late finish would be catastrophic to your up and coming firm. Your decision whether or not to proceed would be based on resource availability and your confidence to be able to complete the works on time, it will also be dependent on what else is currently happing in your organisation and what the overall constantly changing risk profile looks like. Keeping a live risk register can act as a barometer for your organisations ability to manage risk and guide the decision making process of the senior team. In the face of a business strategy to grow sales to £100M, the pressure to take on the supermarket contract may be significant but the potential risks must be fully appreciated before making a decision. There are a number of companies that have gone bust that have cited this poor contract and that poor contract but the poor contracts were never recognised as such until it was too late.

In summary you should constantly monitor what is going on in the market place with your competition and keep making the necessary adjustments. It's a little bit like the concept of boiling a frog, ***please do not try this at home*** but if you placed a frog in a cold pan of water and gradually turned up the heat, it would just stay there until it becomes an ex-frog. This gruesome experiment (or folklore) is a great illustration of the frog not noticing changes to its environment because it is right in the middle of it, it happens gradually over time and by the time it realises it is in trouble it is too late. Do periodic risk reviews where the whole team objectively asseses current reality, this is a key part of ensuring that the industry press in the future are not picking over the remains of your business and asking what went wrong and why did no one in the leadership team notice the seamingly obvious.

9 Selling the vision

"Culture eats strategy for breakfast," Peter Drucker

Now you now have a strategy, you have completed the discovery phase and considered all of your strategic choices and decided on what will give you the competitive advantage in the market. You have then constructed a strategy map and looked at all the requirements for building your people through your Learning and Growth initiatives and you have looked at ways in which you can streamline and improve Internal Processes to better align yourselves to serve the customer. You have all the building blocks in place for a strategy that makes you and your offering unique in the marketplace to improve customer perception through strengthening the customers value proposition. The expected outcomes of all this activity have been modelled and you have compiled your 5 year budgets and forecasts along with a suitably robust risk and opportunities register.

At this point you have a strategy that is capable of winning but it is still a long way from being a winning strategy. You have a great strategy but as I cautioned in the earlier sections of this book, at some point the strategy will have to be sold to the rest of the organisation. If the strategic execution work that needs to be done is closely aligned with the current culture of your business then you are in luck, if the culture needs to change to deliver the strategy this can present you with a whole host of problems that even having a brilliant and profoundly logical strategy, may not be able to be overcome.

Selling the strategy to gain understanding, acceptance and engagement is another fundamental part of the strategic process that you need to get right. Simply arguing logic and the financial benefits will invariably miss the mark with your audience. The strategy is the "what" and the purpose is the "why". When you think about truly successful companies, they have a purpose other than making money. Here are a few notable examples:-

- **Google** – set out to make all the information in the world organised.
- **Disney** – represents family ideals
- **Amazon** – to be the earth's most customer centric company.
- **Southwest Airlines** – the worlds most loved, most flown and most profitable airline.
- **Starbucks** – The premier purveyor of the finest coffee in the world
- **Zappos** – delivering happiness to customers, employees and vendors.
- **Facebook** – giving people the power to build communitiy and bring the world together.
- **Apple** – we design the best personal computers in the world.

- **Microsoft** – to enable people throughout the world to realise their full potential.

Peter Drucker also once said that businesses should plan based on their mission, not their financial goals. When you speak about an organisations mission, you give it a reason for existing in the first place – a basic purpose. If you are guided by a purpose other than money, your decisions are likely to be more in favor of the long term, than in pursuit of in year financial gains.

As with the black art of strategy, I must confess that I used to get confused around the terminology of the cultural descriptors but I suspect that many people do. Purpose, mission, vision, brand story's, values, behaviors and elevator pitches get thrown around in the corporate boardrooms interchangeably and so what I would like to do now is explain how I make sense of each of the elements in turn. Now if you are reading this book as an owner manager of your family firm, please do not skip this section. You may think that you have come so far without all this 'corporate nonsense' and that talking about mission and purpose has no relevance to you. What I would urge is that you stick with it as even though you may not have warm words and platitudes on your office wall, by the very nature that you have a successful business will mean that all of these exist and it can be a useful exercise to produce them to use as a compass for future decision making and as a way of articulating what your company is all about for future employees and customers.

If you think that you do not have a brand then you are mistaken, you have a personal brand and your company has a brand. Brand is a little bit like strategy in so far as you may not actively pay it any attention or think about it but it does exist. As an example your personal brand could be described as what people say about you when you are not in the room or how they would describe you to another person or potential employer. Putting some time and effort into the following exercise with your team will give you tremendous insight into what it is that really matters to your organisation and its stakeholders. The first time I completed the brand pyramid with my senior team not only did it spark some really good debate and reflection where we were and where we were going but the finished result gave us a powerful framework for message discipline and consistency which until that point had been sadly lacking.

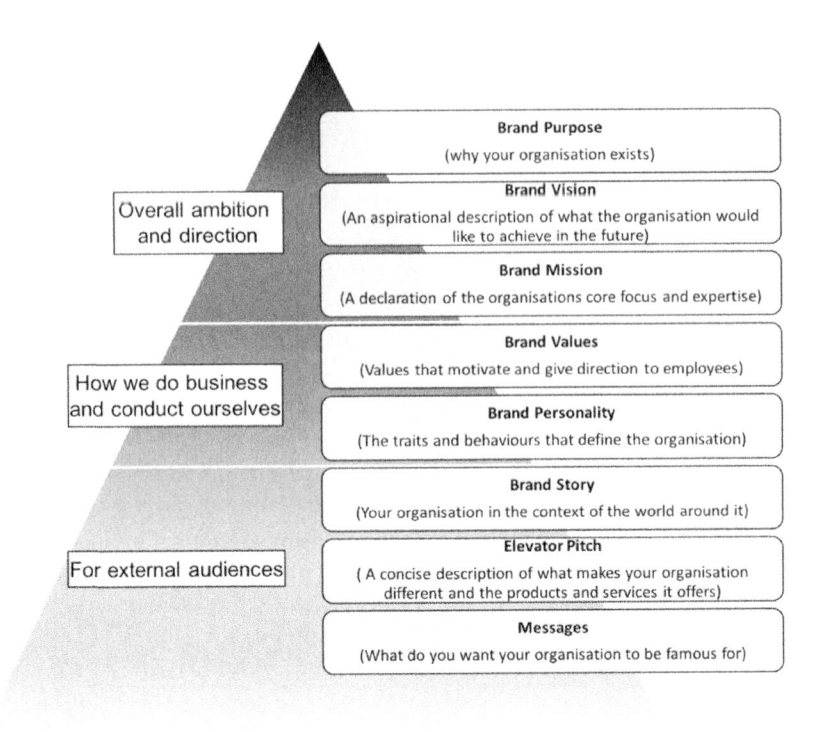

Figure 32 The Brand Pyramid

> *"You can't sell it outside if you can't sell it inside."*
> *— Stan Slap*

Brand Purpose – Why does your business exist? By now I hope you are thinking that its more than just about making money. James Dyson wanted to make a better vacuum cleaner, Henry Ford wanted to bring transportation to the masses. and John F Kennedy wanted to send a man to the moon and return him safely by the end of the decade. Having a purpose gives your business a platform on which to base all your decisions. Sam Walton the founder of Walmart was all about serving the customer and he was driven by altruism and compassion, when he got a good deal on products for their stores they would pass the savings onto the customer rather go for short term increased returns. Do not under estimate the power of purpose to attract the very best people to your organisation.

Brand Vision – this is all about where you want your business to be in the future and it should be inspiring for your customers and your employees alike. For the avoidance of doubt this is not where you say that you want to be at £100M of sales in five years' time. Instead it should be a description of the promised land, what kind of impact will your business have on the world and what will it be like for your employees to be with you on that journey. Your vision should be a vivid description of the future that is time bound and that is potentially only 70% achievable but most importantly it energises everyone in the organisation. John F Kennedy wanted to send a man to the moon and return him safely by the end of the decade. He made that famous speech in May 1961 when America had spent a grand total of 15 minutes in space. The vision that Kennedy launched on that day galvanised a nation and at its peak NASA was employing 400,000 people in pursuit of the vision. As the story goes, President Kennedy was visiting NASA headquarters for the first time, in 1961. While touring the facility, he introduced himself to a janitor who was mopping the toilet floor and asked him what he did at NASA. The janitor replied, "I'm helping put a man on the moon!"

Figure 33 The dream versus the potential reality

Brand Mission – the mission is supposed to reflect your company's core focus and expertise, it is important that you do not fall into a common trap. Anyone reading your mission statement that has a reasonable knowledge of the work you do, should be able to identify your company from its mission statement. A common mistake with mission statements is that they sound too generic, something like this " we are committed to adding value to our customers and working in a safe and sustainable way being excellent at what we do". Reading the two mission statements below however, you could probably hazard a good gues who they are.

"To inspire and nurture the human spirit – one person, one cup and one neighbourhood at a time". – Starbucks Mission Statement

To make, distribute and sell the finest quality ice cream and euphoric concoctions with a continued commitment to incorporating wholesome, natural ingredients and promoting business practices that respect the Earth and the Environment. – Ben & Jerry Mission Statement

Brand Values – Values are a key determinant of culture because core values will determine your company's behaviors. Having strong corporate values makes sure that your go about your business in the right way. Many companies have a set of values, but the very best companies make sure they are interwoven to their culture. It's the 'how they do busines', they use their company values to make the right business decisions even if means compromising short term profitability. The values of the organisation need to be upheld without exception in an environment where everyone in the organisation holds each other to account. When we launched our values in a major construction company a few years ago, our CEO at the time launched the values and advised us never to do anything that we would not want to read about in a newspaper. I think this was very sound advice as often without a moral compass people make the wrong decisions. Here are the values of the failed giant Enron, a careful reminder that there is a world of difference between having values and living values.

Enron's Values - Respect, Integrity, Communication and Excellence

Brand Personality – Your organisational traits and behaviours. Are you approachable problem solvers? Are you an expert authority? Are you fun and innovative? There are some brands out there with very strong personalities such as Ben & Jerry ice cream which is fun innovative with a big social conscience. There are other brands out there such as Lexus and AUDI which are all about engineering excellence.

Brand Story – your business in the the context of the world around it. You could have something like 'we are passionate engineers that are trying to make the world a sustainable and better workplace'. This should be a narrative by which you can be a Thought Leader and enter into conversations with your customers and wider social groups. Having a brand story to support your business and its long terms goals and aspirations is a great way not only to sell to your customers but it will act as a guiding light to attract and retain the kind of talent you are looking for.

Elevator Pitch –this is a short soundbite of information that you would give to a very important customer if you were ever lucky enough for them to step into your otherwise empty elevator hit the ground floor button and politely ask what your company does. It is important to have your elevator pitch ready, polished and drilled. I have worked in some pretty complicated services business and I am always amazed when I overhear people explaining to others what their business does. You can very quickly distinguish between a finely tuned elevator pitch and the unprepared stream of consciousness that goes on for five minutes like some sort of memory quiz on the generation game. I prepared an elevator pitch for our multi services engineering company, it worked across multiple sectors and consequently it was a challenge to reduce the elevator pitch down to something less than a pitch that would only work in the Empire State building but we managed with this little poem. We then got our apprentices to video the pitch and place it on our website to give a more meaningfull overview to our capability and expertise in a simple memorablepitch.

We are the engineers behind the worlds best chocolate
We are the engeineers behind the worlds favourite drink
We are the engineers that help build your motorcars
We are the engineers that can make your factory think!
We keep the warm warm, the cold cold and turn darkness into light.
We are the engineers behind the engineers that help our soldiers fight
We are the engineers!
We are ....

Messages – Your key messages are very important and again these should be well understood by as many people as possible in your organisation.

These should reaffirm what you want to be famous for and what makes your organisation unique and aligned to the key strengths of your strategy. At all points of interaction in the media, at trade shows, in the bar and anywhere else where you can launch into a mini presentation of what your company is all about you need to remember your company's 3 or 4 key messages. For each of your key messages you also need to be able to give real life examples and truth points in support of the messages.

Having a clear and concise brand pyramid (page 89) for you organisation will ensure message consistency and message discipline. Just about the worst thing that can happen on a customer visit is for your long standing customer to say "oh I didn't know that you did that". As an organisation you have to take full responsibility for the ways in which you communicate your brand and it is surprising just how many companies do not have a brand pyramid and leave these important messages to chance.

Clearly defining what your company is all about and articulating the vision of where you want your company to be in the future is fundamentally important not only to your customers but to the people that make up the culture in your own organisation. The launch of a new strategic vision will invariably require a certain amount of change, I would be very suspicious of a strategic review process where the net result is to declare "steady as she goes, all is well".

Knowing that culture can eat strategy for breakfast should not be taken lightly and ignoring the culture is one of the two deadly sins of why strategic execution fails.

1. CEO's under estimate the cultural inertia and the sheer amount of effort it takes to chieve a culture change.
2. Everyone involved in the strategy underestimates the amount of time and discipline it takes to deliver a successful strategy.

I will address the second deadly sin later in the book but first lets discuss culture. When I thought about writing this book, just like looking at a good strategy I wanted to produce something unique, I was conscious that there is no shortage of books on strategy but what there is a shortage of books assisting to overcome cultural inertia and execution to ensure successful delivery. I very much suspect that the reason for this is that the study of culture and how to change it does not lend itself to a book full of tangible models and four box grids. Culture is very much about the intangibles and the unmeasurable even though there are surveys to try and identify cultural characteristics the subject matter is a bit of a minefield.

Rather than shy aware from the minefield lets go headlong into looking at curtural change and say goodbye at this point in the book to the clearly defined four box grids.

10 Culture

"Growing a culture requires a good storyteller. Changing a culture requires a persuasive editor."
— Ryan Lilly

There are over 120 definitions of culture with the more popular and generally accepted ones relating to the workplace citing the way we do things around here (Deal & Kennedy, 1982). Definitions of "organisational culture" are almost as numerous as those of "culture"— a 1998 study identified 54 different definitions within the academic literature between 1960 and 1993. I will start this chapter by giving you a super concentrated get up to speed quickly delve into cultural writers on organisations that I think will add value and give you a flavoursome overview of the complex world of culture and how to try and change it. One helpful though general definition offered by Edgar Schein of Massachusetts Institute of Technology (MIT) is that organisational culture is:-

"A pattern of shared basic assumptions that the group learned as it solved its problems of external adaptation and internal integration, that has worked well enough to be considered valid and, therefore, to be taught to new members as the correct way to perceive, think, and feel in relation to those problems" (Schein, 1992)

Schein also talks about the three distinct levels of organisational culture, one of which being artefacts which are visible to an observer outside of the organisation such as architecture, furniture, dress code and office jokes. Then he describes the espoused values and beliefs of the organisation that need to be evidenced and reinforced over time by the leaders and participants. Finally he describes the deeply held implicit assumptions at the organisational level that are formed by historical responses to the businesses activity.

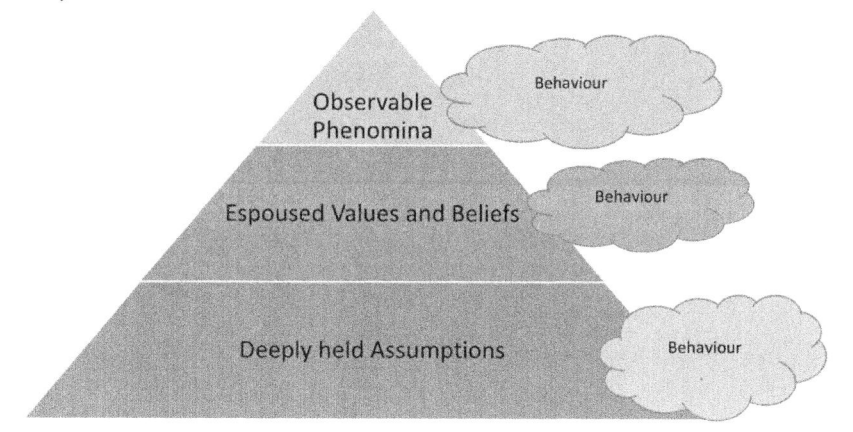

Figure 34 Adapted from Schein's 3 levels of Culture

Founding and early growth cultural development comes from the founders and their assumptions and the these leaders at the early stages of the organisation would recruit people with the same values, beliefs and assumptions as their own. The proposition from Schein on founding and early growth is that changing a culture in a successful business at such an early stage would be met with a lot of resistance, as the founders are still present and that they were the primary cultural creators and the psychological glue that holds the organisation together. Another way to think about this organisational glue is to think of it as your cultural immune system that is there to defend the current practices and systems and it will try to attack and destroy anything that tries to change it. To take this immune system theory a step further think about someone who is getting a new heart, even though the heart transplant is being undertaken to save the patient's life, the natural instinct of the body's immune system is to reject it. Logical argument alone is not good enough to change a culture, a systemic process and the battle for hearts and minds needs to take the majority of the employees past the tipping point of organisational inertia and move it culturally to the better place.

Deal and Kennedy (1982) defined organisational culture as "the way things get done around here". Early change efforts may show a promising start but any visible changes in cultural performance need to be viewed with a dose of scepticism as this may give you a false positive. The cultural glue of the organisation also has an element of elasticity that is locked into the organisational memory and often change programmes fail as leaders see a change and then celebrate the success too early and think that the change programme is over. A better way of thinking about the real culture in an organisation is "the way things are done around here, when we think nobody is looking".

Van Den Steen (2010) believed that culture comes from a collection of shared history and experience from which people draw a sense of meaning. This is very much in keeping with the purpose, and brand stories from the pyramid.

Shared History → Shared Experience → Shared Assumptions →
- Meaning
- Organisational comfort zone
- Stability

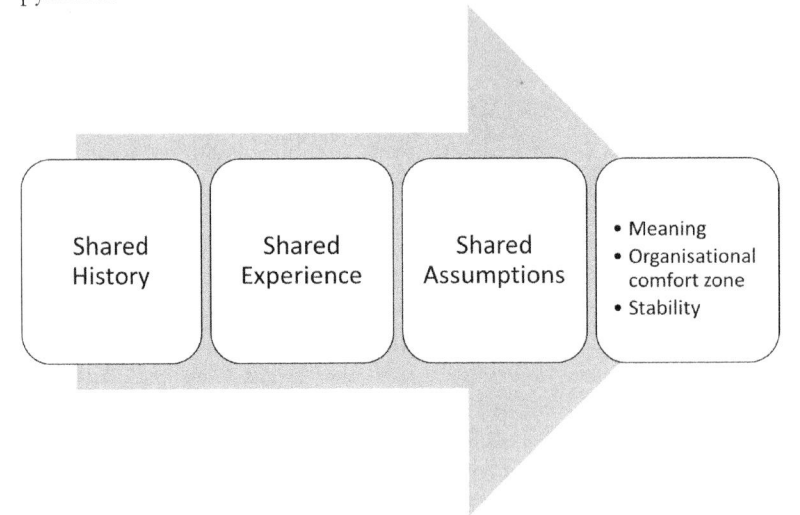

Figure 35 Adopted from Van Den Steen 2010

There are lots of studies on culture and some writers seem to favour a hypothesis that the culture cannot be changed and that any attempts of cultural change by a new CEO would only result in the CEO being changed in the process. Other writers say that culture can be changed and this is the doctrine that I subscribe too but it takes a certain type of leader to make it happen. Transactional leaders tend to operate within the constraints of the existing culture and transformational leaders frequently work towards changing the culture in line with their vision. The best transformational leaders develop skills that enable them to alter aspects of their culture in order to improve organisational performance. In his book 21st Century People Leadership (Stitt, 2010) argues that leaders need to be truly connected to the people in their organisation to drive and shape the culture.

In his book the Fifth Discipline, Senge (1990) talks about the power of leadership connection and culture, he notes that among the tribes of northern Natal the most common greeting is "sawu bona" which means "I see you" if you're a member of the tribe, you say "sikhona", or "I am here". It's as if you do not exist until you are seen. In their book Made to Stick, Chip & Dan Heath (2007) point out that when most CEO's take to the podium they have on average 30 years of immersion in the conventions and logic of business language and in most cases the language just does not connect in a way that can materially impact culture. When John F Kennedy asked congress for an extra $1.7 billion for his space programme, he really connected; "I believe that this nation should commit itself to achieving the goal, before this decade is out, of landing a man on the moon and return him safely to Earth", he said which was a great speech that resonated with a worldwide audience. For it to stick the Heaths (2007) insist that the messaging has to be simple, unexpected, concrete and credible. In his book Brain Rules, Medina (2014) observed that we process things in a certain order (1) emotions first (2) then meaning (3) then detail. In changing a culture people are emotionally charged either through excitement or fear, Medina counsels that any leader wanting to change a culture needs to let the emotions in and let them be heard.

So we have created a strategy looking at hard data and sound business logic but in order for the strategy to succeed we have to convince irrational and emotional human beings that this will be a journey worth taking. Logical argument alone is never enough for cultural change, you have to appeal to the hopes and fears of your employee base as this is the only way you can get them to move in the desired direction. You may be a little concerned at the use of the word fear as frightened employees do not make for happy and engaged employees but dependent on what strategic challenges you are facing there may good reason to know the full implications of doing nothing. I often think it is easier to change cultures in a turnaround situation than it is in an already successful organisation looking for additional growth. The failing business will generally already be sold on the need for dramatic change and they implicitly realise that there is a real burning platform to do things differently. The already successful business looking to grow to the next level will often think doing more of the same will get them there. Whichever situation you find yourself in there are some very specific attributes of cultural change that you must attend to in support of your strategic change programme to avoid becoming one of the 70% failure statistics.

The following illustration is adopted from Schein's work on cultural design and transformation and could be used to illustrate the areas of focus for the leadership team to shape the culture by design in support of the strategy. I did warn you that the four box grids maybe a little thin on the ground in this section.

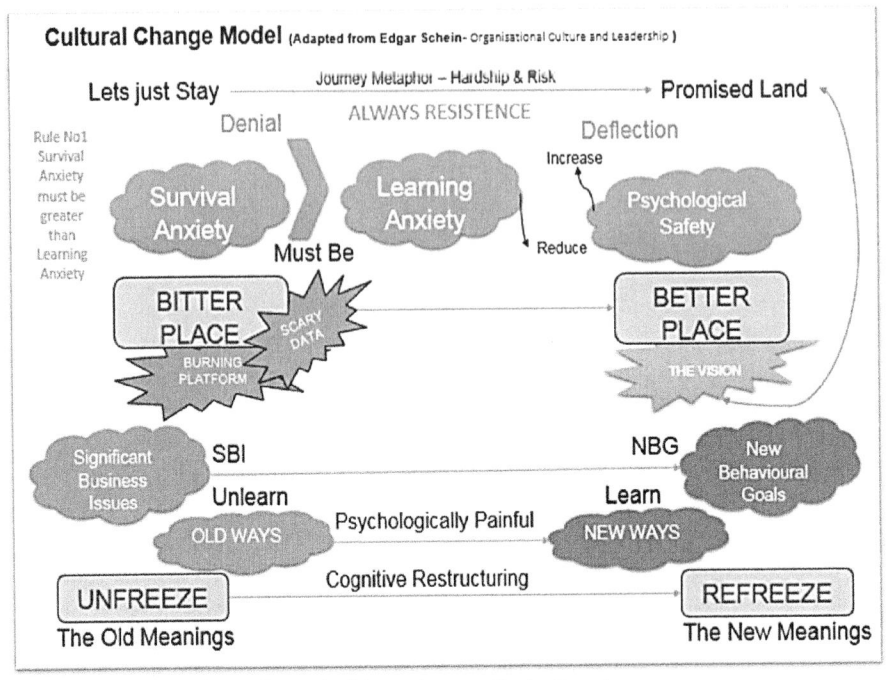

Cultural Change Model (Adapted from Edgar Schein- Organisational Culture and Leadership)

Figure 36 Moving cultures from the bitter place to the better place

The Bitter Place – As good as your strategy is you still need to have a compelling reason for your culture to change. As the leader you need to create a burning platform to let your people know that staying put culturally is not a long term viable option.

"If you want things to stay the same, things are going to have to change", Anon.

Sometimes changes in your competitive marketplace happen slowly over time which can make the creation of a burning platform for your people all the more difficult but please remember the frog experiment from the previous chapter. You will have access to the scary data showing a reduction in sales, losses in market share, the take up of alternative products and technologies. Your people will need to experience survival anxiety associated with standing culturally still. This messaging of course needs to be handled sensitively and is best delivered and countered in the same presentation on what needs to happen to get to the better place. The wrong thing to do here is say something along the lines of we are receiving reports that we have just struck an iceberg and we are assessing the situation and will get back to you as soon as we have figured out what we have to do. Instead you need to be ready with what exactly you intend to do and reassure the audience of your confidence that by doing this now, the future (better place) will be all the more comfortable for their long term success. Yes as leaders we want to protect our people, but only being prepared to share good news can lull your people and subsequently culture into a false sense of security that can ultimately lead to its own downfall.

The Better Place – As a visionary leader it is all about painting an emotional picture for your people so they feel that the journey will be worth it. As well as sharing the scary data and creating a burning platform under the current cultural paradigm, you also have to work simultaneously on selling them on the promised land or the better place. There will be a certain amount of learning anxiety associated with the cultural changes that need to take place and the important thing is to ensure that the survival anxiety associated with doing nothing is greater than the learning anxiety associated with the journey to the better place. The required cultural change to support the strategy will deliver the long term success and offer your people the psychological safety of job security and greater opportunity for future development. Remember this is about hearts and minds so it's all about what it will feel like to work in your business in the future. Selling your people on your vision to be the largest provider of office stationery may not quite hit the mark but if say when that goal is achieved that you will be moving to a new purpose built state of the art facility and you intend to launch a management development programme to grow future leaders from inside the current workforce, then now you are closer to the dreams and aspirations that may more closely match your employees vision for the promised land.

Sometimes leaders have to be disruptive in a way that challenges the status quo of a culture to get the changes they want. To take a classic example from the automotive sector, in 1908 Henry Ford gave his motor company a big problem. He said they would make it possible for most households in the US to buy a car. This was at a time when only 2% of the population could afford one and cars cost $1500. By 1924 with his disruptive problem challenge to his business this subsequently drove innovation and through the development of a production line approach they had successfully reduced the price to just $290.

As cultural change is quite literally like trying to turn a super tanker you need to set up short feedback loops across the organisation and create a deliberate and systemic approach to keeping your people on that cultural journey.

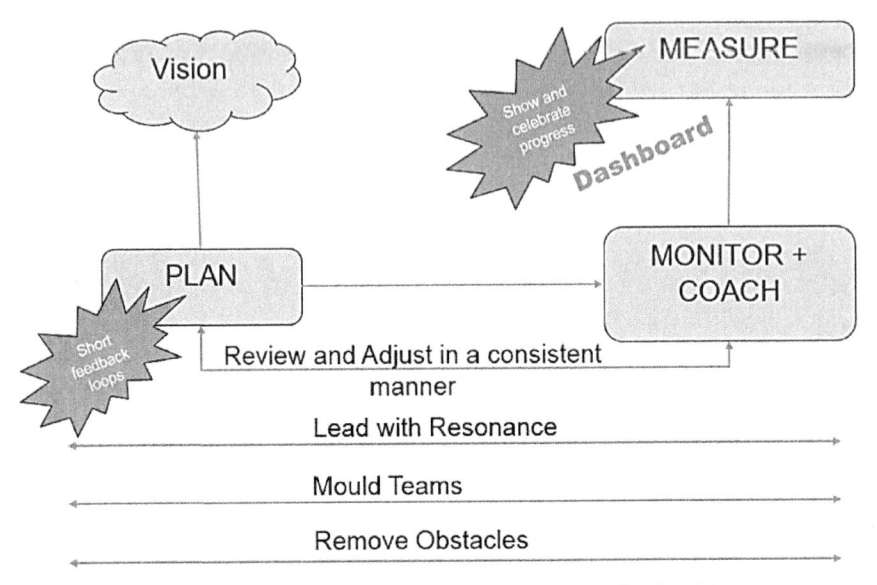

Figure 37 Leading cultural change through coaching and short feedback loops

In terms of delivering the vision and shaping the culture it is incumbent initially on the leadership team but then subsequently through the management teams to create strong plans with regular monitoring and coaching for performance through short feedback loops. These short feedback loops are essentially the checking in and adjustments against expected outcomes, which are generally established via measurement. The Plan, Do, Check, Act method of constantly reviewing progress is a good discipline to make sure you keep moving your change efforts forward. To this I would also add celebrating success at every opportunity. By celebrating success everytime your new way of doing things around here is generating results, this creates a positive reinforcing mechanism and creates truth points to support the change initiative which will encourage the believers and help to sway a skeptical majority. One of the most important things to remember is to keep open the lines of communication about the change initiative and constantly look for ways to keep up the conversation with your employees to reinforce the message. CEO's generally under communicate their change initiatives by a factor of 10X, they think because we told everyone about our new strategy at the December employee away day, that everyone in the business will still be on message the following February. The quality of the communication can only really be measured by the reaction you get but in general you should aim to look at your initial communications plan and then multiply the activity by a factor of 10. This may seem excessive but when you are absolutely getting fed up of hearing yourself pushing the message work on the assumption that 10% of the organisation will remember the message. Unless you have the luxury of something as compelling as going to the moon, your message around your change activity will need all the help it can get and quality and quantity of messaging in equal heavy doses will go a long way.

11 Execution

"We have a strategic plan. It's called doing things." – Herb Kelleher Founder & CEO of Southwest Airlines

Ok so this is where the rubber hits the road. I am not sure if they have changed the MBA syllabus since I did mine, but this next bit is what they did not teach me at business school. Subsequently that is probably why 70% of strategies fail, it is because they stumble when it comes to execution. I think part of the problem with execution is that its right at the end of the planning and selling phase. By this time the senior team have been living and breathing the new strategy for so long that they feel like they are already well into the program. At risk of stating the painstakingly obvious there is no point in having a brilliant strategy that works perfectly in theory unless it actually works in practice. So many great strategies get to this point which is like digging a 100 foot gold mine and then giving up three feet from gold. Sticking with the analogy, the last three feet is potentially the hardest. This is about having the shear force of will, discipline and determination to overcome the tremendous amount of inertia that exists within the organisation, it's about changing behaviours, overcoming resistance and not only thinking but
doing thinks differently.

The good news is that we have done everything right up until now, we may have even got the most resistant of audiences in the organisation to a point where they are enthused about the journey to the better place in pursuit of the vision. Surely then we will now be unstoppable but the problem is that this state of upbeat euphoria is about as long lasting as a typical new year's resolution which can be an exercise of hope over experience. What we need now is organisational discipline. Before I let you in on secrets to getting the execution right, first of all I will share a scenario that is representative of some of my earlier experiences of strategic delivery.

Image it is now 12 months since the launch and we have all returned to the beautiful country hotel for an update on progress against the strategy.

As the morning progresses there are a couple of disturbing thoughts that pass through your mind, the first is that you cannot believe that a year has passed since launch day and the second is a concern that the facilitator will put you on the spot and ask exactly how you are getting on with the bold and ambitious plans that you recall the room cheering and whooping too the previous year. The fundamental problem here we think is time, as enthusiastic as we were when we left the hotel the year before, we got back to the office and were hit by what Chris McChesney et al in their book "The Four Disciplines of Execution", call the whirlwind in their study of why strategies fail. This is the enormous amount of effort and grunge just to keep up with the real work of the day job. We work twelve hour days without taking lunch and in what feels like the blink of any eye a year has gone by and the strategic delivery is no further forward.

The problem though is not time it's the prioritisation of time. Every human being on the planet is blessed with exactly 24 hours a day and some are better at getting stuff done than others. Time is an abstract concept, it cannot be managed, it cannot be controlled, spent, slowed down or saved but how we allocate and prioritise what we call time makes all of the difference. Instead of thinking about time, it is better to think about priorities. This way you will be much more effective at getting the execution part right. The problem with strategy is that it is not urgent and so the strategic actions have to battle with endless urgent priorities, text messages ringing phones that already make up 99.9% of your exhausting day job. Another problem with strategy is that it is also not going to deliver any benefits in the immediate short term and as a society we are all addicted to now and the instant gratification that we get from a job well done. The distance between your strategic actions and being able to see any tangible benefits are generally so far removed that the more pressing jobs that give us immediate feedback get our priority. We get a kick out of putting fires out and let's face it being a fireman is much more glamourous than being a fire prevention officer.

Executing strategy is like everything else worthwhile in life, it takes commitment, dedication and discipline. It's about having the discipline to defer gratification of the daily self-worth of being a fireman for playing the longer game which could generate a significantly more profound effect by for your organisations future. This is where the discipline comes in because as a leader or senior manager you have to make a daily judgement call between being a fire fighter and fire prevention officer. If you declare at your strategy meeting that from this day forward you are only going to be focused on the long term strategy of the organisation it's analogous to running into a burning building to raise awareness on smoke alarms. So it is very important that you become aware of how you are prioritising your time so that can deliver on your strategy. Your prioritisation on a daily basis needs to be context specific but leaving this judgement call to individuals then falls back on the daily discipline to make the right choices and defer instant gratification of the day job.

Health Plan

IT TAKES
4 WEEKS
FOR YOU TO SEE YOUR BODY CHANGING

IT TAKES
8 WEEKS
FOR YOUR FRIENDS AND FAMILY

IT TAKES
12 WEEKS
FOR THE REST OF THE WORLD

KEEP GOING

Strategic Plan

IT TAKES
40 WEEKS
FOR YOU TO SEE YOUR CHANGING

IT TAKES
60 WEEKS
FOR YOUR CUSTOMERS

IT TAKES
120 WEEKS
FOR THE REST OF THE WORLD

KEEP GOING

Figure 38 Strategy and weight loss are simplicity on the far side of complexity

Losing weight and executing strategy are both exercises in personal mastery:-

Losing Weight – you have decided that to secure your long term health you are going to lose weight and get in great shape. You make a commitment to go to the gym three times a week and eat a sensible balanced diet with the right amount of protein, fibre, carbohydrates and fats. You have a 52 week plan and you are motivated as your doctor has warned you that things need to change for your long term quality of life. The first few weeks are great, you stick to your plan and although there are no immediately measureable benefits you feel a sense of accomplishment that you are doing the right thing. As time goes by, the early sense of accomplishment diminishes and so do your weekly trips to the gym, things happen in your life that disrupt your gym routine for a couple of weeks. On top of all this you are bombarded with a daily barrage of advertising from the food industry and every day you have to get up and try and behave and stay strong until bedtime. With all of the daily temptations, willpower alone is never enough to overcome the 24/7 pressure to let go and get the instant gratification that by now you are sure that you deserve. A year passes and you are right back where you started but you feel in good company as nearly 70% of the adult population are overweight. You resolve that next year will be different and this time you are determined

Executing Strategy - you have decided that to secure your long term future you are going to grow sales and get in great shape. You make a commitment to go and visit your customers three times a week and balance your time between competing daily priorities and making sure this includes development of long term customer relationships. You have a 52 week plan and you are motivated as your CFO has warned you that things need to change for the long term health of the business. The first few weeks are great, you stick to your plan and although there are no immediately measureable benefits you feel a sense of accomplishment that you are doing the right thing. As time goes by, the early sense of accomplishment diminishes and so do your weekly visits to your customers, things happen at work that disrupt your customer visits for a couple of weeks. On top of all this you are bombarded with a daily barrage of employee relations issues, ringing telephones and urgent emails and every day you have to get up and try and make time for you customers. With all of the daily temptations, willpower alone is never enough to overcome the 24/7 pressure to let go and get the instant gratification of putting out fires. A year passes and you are right back where you started but you feel in good company as nearly 70% of all strategies fail. You resolve that next year will be different and this time you are determined.

So what you need is a way of turning determination into disciplined strategic execution which like making regular visits to the gym is far easier said than done. I recall a particularlary busy period in my life when I discovered a new way of looking at how I manage and prioritise my time. I had a young family, I was working full time and studying in my spare time which was generally carved out of when I should have been sleeping. Now I look back to this time when I thought that my life was busy and out of control and it was 1994 some twelve months before I had received my first ever e-mail. Life before email and mobile phones was busy enough but by the mid 1990's thing were changing at an increasingly eye watering rate that meant for just about all of us, the prospect of being bored which seemed to be a regular pastime as a child would be a condition that had been condemned to the past. Little did we know that following the birth of the internet, it would create the the biggest shift in our lifes and economy since the industrial revolution. I witnessed the birth of the internet first hand and as part of my studies in technology at the time I was required to get myself an internet account and so I subscribed to a company called Netscape who were revolutionary in bringing the internet to the masses. Way back in 1995 Netscape gave me access to 23,500 web sites which were fairly unsophisticated but that was probably for the best considering I had to access them with a 28,800kps modem attached to the telephone line. Pictures would literally load a line at a time and at that time and although people were hyping the internet and what it might do for us in the future it was quite a leap for the imagination just 23 years ago. The rest as they say is history and due to the explosion of the internet by the end of March 2016 the total number of registered websites had grown to 4.62 Billion all of which are trying to grab our attention. In a world that is now collectively suffering from attention deficit disorder, how we choose to allocate our precious time is becoming even more critical. In business we hire people for their skills at multi-tasking in the hope that they can cope with what feels like processing requests and information analgous to trying to take a drink of water from a fire hose. We are all addicted to now and we are in a constant state of distraction. Have you ever been working away on your computer and you hear that familiar ping that you have mail but you are right in the flow of things so you carry on what you are doing. Two minutes later you get a phone call from the sender asking if you have seen their e-mail, you tell them no because you were just in the middle of something and then they proceed to read the e-mail out to you and 30 minutes later you finally manage to get them off the phone.

THE AGGREGATION OF MARGINAL GAINS

At the 2012 Olympics the British cycling team won 8 from a total of 18 gold medals up for grabs across all the cycling events. The team cycling coach David Brailsford was as meticulous as you would expect from any Olympic team coach and as well as getting his athletes to their peak physical condition, he would also have to get them to peak mental condition to put up with the intense pressure of the event and competing on home turf in the spectacular Olympic velodrome. As well as mentally conditioning the athletes as winners he had a unique way of not only giving his team a measurable time advantage but this would help build their confidence and psychological edge over the competition. He developed the concept of marginal gains whereby he and his team would do hundreds of little things each designed to make the athletes and their bikes go fractions of a second faster. He took the athletes own mattresses to the Olympic village to make sure they got the best night's sleep, they wiped down the bikes tyres with alcohol to remove all traces of dust to reduce friction. The athletes would wear heated shorts to keep their thigh muscles at the optimal performance temperature in between heats. All of the marginal gains from the hundreds of micro improvements may well of added up to a half a second advantage in real terms as well as the psychological advantage that this obsessive attention to detail would give the athletes. At the start of each race the athletes would feel confident that they had done absolutely everything to squeeze out every last ounce of performance which of course is a great position to be in pschologically at the beginning of a race and the rest of course is history.

I appreciate that in the majority of our business undertakings you do not measure performance in fractions of a second but if you take the concept of marginal gains and apply it to a typical day at the office you will be surprised of what can be achieved. There is a special day each year when you turn into the most efficient turbo charged version of yourself and that is the day before your annual holiday. You have just one more day at the office and your to do list is stretching off into the distant horizon and you have to leave at 5pm as you have not packed yet and you are catching the 10pm flight. You leave the house that morning knowing that whatever does not get done will just have to wait until you get back but everything on your list is important. You put your game face on and for the rest of the day you walk 20% faster around the office and your colleagues instinctively know that you are on a mission. You are not rude or unpolite but you are efficient and on a deadline and nothing is going get in your way, you want that feeling of being at a straight edge when you get on that plane. By 3pm in the afternoon in the afternoon you are well on your way to achieving your goal and even though you have literally not stopped since you got in the door that morning you feel more energised than ever, you also notice that your efficiency drive seems to have been contagious as your colleagues seem to have tuned into your frequency. At the end of the day you put on your out of office and you cannot quite believe what you have accomplished. That was just one day, imagine how much you could get done if you approached each day as if it was your last day before your vacation.

Figure 39 The power of the self-imposed deadline for getting things done!

So first let's have a look at how you are allocating your time. The illustration below is adapted from Stephen R. Covey's excellent time management book "First things first". This is one of his seven habits of highly effective people that shot him to fame in 1989 and has sold him well over 20 million books since. I remember reading the book and thinking that it was groundbreaking as all the time management books prior to this seemed to be focused on thin slicing your day and being efficient with people by saying "no" to their requests or creating ellaborate tick lists and to do's that you could cross off and get a sense of accomplishment. The fist things first approach however changed the way you look at time management and it focussed on sacrificing the unimportant for the important. It is not about getting everything done but getting the most important things done first.

BUILDING A WINNING BUSINESS STRATEGY

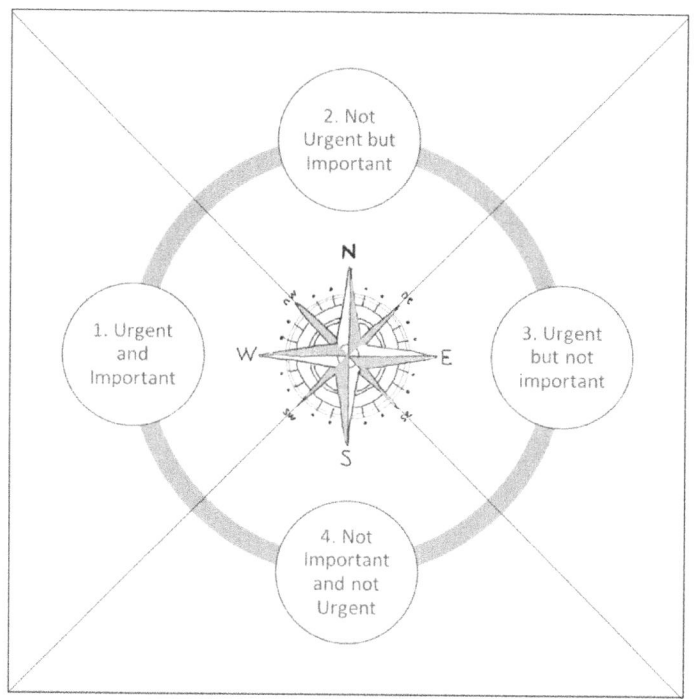

Figure 40 Stephen R Covey's - First things first -Time management quadrants

1. **Urgent and important** – This is the quadrant where we take care of those priority jobs, the demands of the customer, the tender deadlines and this is where we deal with the daily crisis of putting fires out and keeping the wheels turning. This is where we feel like we spend most of our working life. The urgent important quadrant however, is not where strategy happens because if strategy were urgent and important more of it would get done.
2. **Not urgent but important** – This is quadrant 2 activity and this is where we spend time on the strategy and all of the important but not urgent things in life. This is true North, Stephen Covey and his team talk about using a compass not a clock. Your true North should be the magnetic pull back to the truly important things so you don't end up lost or simply helping other people get to where they want to. Whenever you are not dealing with the urgent and important, your compass should flip back to your work on quadrant 2 activity. This is for working on strategy, self-development, reflection, going to the gym, spending time with loved ones and giving something back to the community.
3. **Urgent but not important** – these activities may be important to someone else but not to you and what you would like to achieve.

This is where the phone rings and someone is trying to sell you something or there is a knock at the door. These are things that disrupt and demand your attention and if you are not careful can end up completley hijacking your day.

4. **Not urgent and not important** – this is the Monday morning review of what happened at the weekend on the football pitch, this is the untangling of that big ball of paper clips on your desk. Now I'm not suggesting that office socialising and a tidy desk are not important, but this is all about balance and appropriateness. If you have no time for activity in quadrant 1 or 2 because you are too busy debating the off side rule, in the context of this book I would say you have a problem.

"Things that matter most must never be at the mercy of things that matter least." — Johann Wolfgang von Goethe.

If you have a clear set of priorities these should be the things that you plan and allocate time for. This is a concept called putting the big rocks in first which is a take on a classic time management experiment. For the experiment you take an empty jar and another jar about two thirds its size full of sand. You get a collection of pebbles of different sizes and you ask a participant to tip the sand from the smaller jar into the larger jar and once they have done this you challenge them to put all of the pebbles into the now three quarters full jar of sand and place the lid firmly shut. As the volunteer gets down to the last couple of pebbles they struggle to get the top of the pebbles below the lid line and cannot physically get the lid on the jar.

Now if you repeat the experiment this time you get them to "put the big rocks in first", when this is done then they simply tip the sand into the jar and it finds its way into all the crevices between the pebbles. This time the volunteer can smooth out the top of the sand and place the lid on the jar. The learning in this comes from the associated metaphor that the big rocks are your life priorities, working on the strategy and the mission, time with your family, helping the community, learning and development, friends, socialising and keeping fit. The sand represents the noise of everyday life such as watching TV, checking Facebook, ringing phones and responding to emails. If you do not make sure that you put the big rocks in your weekly planner first, the sand will run in and fill all of the available time and sooner

BUILDING A WINNING BUSINESS STRATEGY

or later you will struggle on keeping commitments with your family or failing in delivering on your strategy at work.

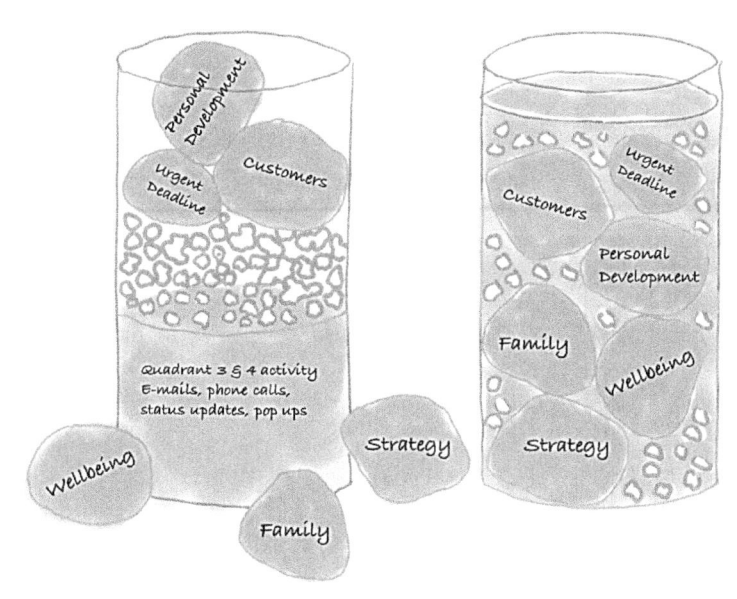

Figure 41 Put the big rocks in first

Putting the big rocks in your diary and making sure you resist all temptation to move them will allocate the time necessary for working actively on delivering your results. On the next corporate away day when all of the team are sat in silence and hoping not to be singled out for updating the room on where they have got to on their plan progress you will be in a position to shine. Your colleagues will stare on in amazement at how you have found the time to get so much done but of course it is not about finding the time it is about prioritising the time to work on the important and not just the urgent. In time because you are working on the strategy the amount of work that ends up as urgent becomes less and this can happen for two distinct reasons. Firstly your strategic outputs head off those sales drives or cost cutting crisis projects that arise periodically in companies with no active strategy and secondly in your disciplined attempt to spend time on quadrant 2 strategic work, you have become much better at delegating the more urgent work and have resisted all temptation to role your sleeves up and get stuck in just like the good old days. It is about being Emotionally Intelligent enough to defer the gratification of putting fires out

113

and getting bogged down in the thick end of thin things and keeping to your true North by working on the strategic deliverables.

Being busy should never be an excuse for not delivering on strategic objectives but time and time again colleagues collectively let each other off the hook and they all fail together. It will only take a few people in an organisation to practice putting the big rocks in first and this will act as a positive and influential example and in fact if you approach your weekly plan in this way you will still manage to get everything done including the strategy. In his brilliant book "Rich Dad Poor Dad", author Robert Kiyosaki came up with a fantastically simple concept about what makes rich people rich and poor people poor. If you think about spending time in the same way as spending money this works equally well.

Rich People = Spend what they do not save

Poor People = Save what they do not spend

Using this and applying it to time management :-

Successful time rich people = Quadrant 2 first then allocate what's left

Time poor people = Spare time allocated to Quadrant 2

All strategic activity could be classified as quadrant 2 and if you only allocate spare time to quadrant 2 this will never happen and that is why 70% of all strategies fail. Put the big rocks in first associated with quadrant 2 activity and resist all temptation to move them from your diary . At the product innovation company 3M, employees are instructed to spend 15% of their working life in quadrant 2 working on pet projects and the success of two such projects came together and gave the world Post It notes. Imagine what you could achieve in your own company if at the start of each 40 hour week you allocated 6 hours (15%) of your time to work on the future of your company. You may well be reading this and thinking that you do indeed plan your week by allocating sufficient time to work on strategic delivery but then of course something more important comes along.

This is a supposed transcript of a radio conversation between a US Naval ship and Canadian authorities off the coast of Newfoundland.

US SHIP: Please divert your course 0.5 degrees to the South to avoid a collision.

CANADIAN REPLY: Recommend you divert YOUR course 15 degrees to the South to avoid a collision.

US SHIP: This is the Captain of the US Navy Ship. I say again, divert YOUR course.

CANADIAN REPLY: No, I say again, divert YOUR course!

US SHIP: THIS IS THE USS MISSOURI. WE ARE A LARGE BATTLESHIP OF THE US NAVY. DIVERT YOUR COURSE NOW OR WE WILL TAKE APPROPRIATE AND DRASTIC MEASURES!!!!

CANADIAN REPLY: This is the lighthouse. Your call.

Once you have put the quadrant 2 rocks into your weekly planner try and view them as extremely large rocks with lighthouses on and everything else as boats. The temptation to remove and re-schedule the none urgent can sometimes be overwhelming and that is why successful strategic execution is so uncommon. These lighthouses are literally beacons of hope that your company's future will be a brighter one. Share the story of the lighthouse and the USS Missouri with your team, explain that strategic activity (quadrant 2) will now be diarised as lighthouse activity. When your team embrace the concept of these lighthouse meetings it will raise the importance of the strategic delivery and it very quickly becomes taboo to try and re-schedule a lighthouse meeting and this creates a collective accountability for the team to prioritise and deliver the strategy together.

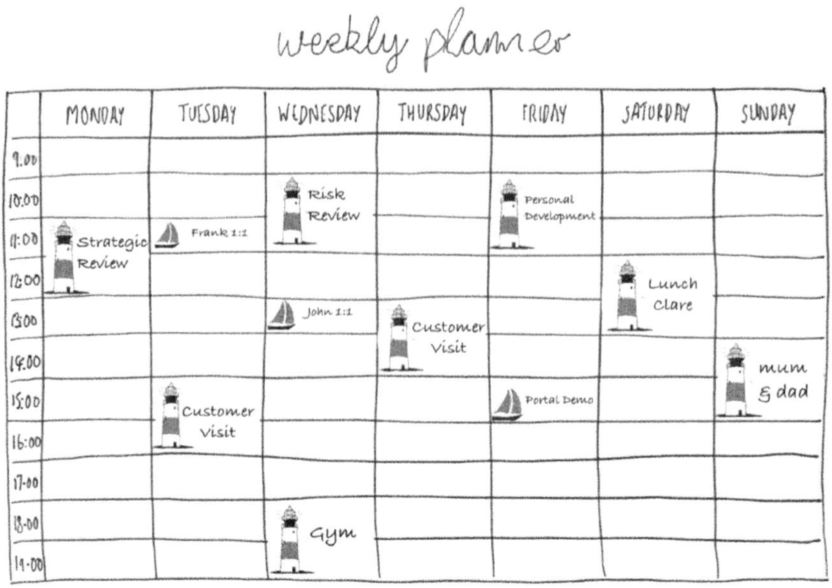

weekly planner

	MONDAY	TUESDAY	WEDNESDAY	THURSDAY	FRIDAY	SATURDAY	SUNDAY
9.00							
10:00			🗼 Risk Review		🗼 Personal Development		
11:00	🗼 Strategic Review	⛵ Frank 1:1					
12:00						🗼 Lunch Clare	
13:00			⛵ John 1:1	🗼 Customer Visit			
14:00							🗼 mum & dad
15:00		🗼 Customer Visit			⛵ Portal Demo		
16:00							
17:00							
18:00			🗼 Gym				
19:00							

Figure 42 Boats and lighthouses approach to time management

FOCUS ON THE WILDLY IMPORTANT

So now you have prioritised the time to work on strategy, make sure that you are working on the things that are going deliver the biggest benefit for your time invested. This is where you could look at your raise and create elements that you compiled during the discovery phase to support service improvements which could be about building better relationships with key customers or making vital system improvements. As time is a precious resource you need to consider the wildly important goals that you need to achieve and these are the ones that are so fundamental to your strategic success that if you do not accomplish them, then nothing else matters. The problem that we have in business is in recognising the important from the wildly import. Of course everything we do in business is important because we would not spend any time working on the un-necessary so we end up with a shopping list of 30 S.M.A.R.T objectives and try and deliver on them all. The problem is that we end up overwhelmed and then do not accomplish any of them or we try and at least achieve some success so we go after the proverbial low hanging fruit but miss the wildly important goals that would add the greatest value to our purpose and direction.

Often you will see role profiles that are looking for candidates that are good at multi-tasking or candidates in interviews will freely offer up their ability to multitask as one of their strengths. The word multi-tasking is derived from a computing term which literally means that the microprocessor brain divides and thin slices its time between activity. You will have noticed that your smartphone or computer starts to slow down considerably when you have too many applications open and if you actually want to get something done you will close down the windows and the applications in the background that are not as important as the one you are working on. Your multi-tasking expert will work diligently all year by starting early and finishing late, they walk 20% faster around the office and always look like they are on a mission. At the end of the year in their performance appraisal you review progress against each of their objectives and they have achieved 80% in every single one of them. This is a tremendous effort but they may have fallen short of some Wildly Important goals that needed to be completed 100% or nothing else mattered from a business perspective. If this person was a lifeguard and she has been throwing 80ft ropes to people drowning 100ft from the shore all year you would have some dead bodies on your hands and it will be little comfort that she has also completed 80% of the new timetable for the swimming lessons. Unless you are very clear on the Wildly Important goals, people will choose to work on the merely important and sometimes this is not quite good enough. There is a time and a place for multitasking and there is a time and a place for doing one thing at a time with excellence. Taking air traffic controllers as an example, they are mindful that they may have several aircraft circling but they are committed to landing one plane at a time with excellence or nothing else matters.

Figure 43 There's a time and a place for multitasking

A LINE OF SIGHT TO THE WILDLY IMPORTANT

In order to cascade meaningful objectives right the way though the organisation you will have to create objectives that are given out at the top and are designed to deliver on the companies top goals for the measurement period. This could involve giving different departments their own wildly important goals but it is important that the various departments understand how their Wildly Important Goals (W.I.Gs) contribute to the overall W.I.Gs of the business. Taking the President Kennedy and the washroom janitor example that we used earlier, this would probably be the exception as going to moon would evoke such a sense of deep and profound meaning to every one of the 460,000 people involved in the space programme that no further interpretation or levels of perspective would be necessary.

Unfortunately we do not all have the privilege in business to be involved in something as inspirational as the space race so we need to be a little more deliberate on how we set goals to inspire and motivate people. One of the common mistakes that CEO's make is thinking that their wildly important goal of growing revenues and increasing EBITDA (Earnings Before Interest Tax Depreciation and Amortization) will be met with the same enthusiasm in all departments. The W.I.G ladder follows a similar format to the strategy map but focuses on the desired outputs that are meaningful at the organisational and departmental levels. This is important because if the CEO stands up and says the most important goals we have this year are to grow revenue and EBITDA by 20% then the rest of the organisation needs to understand exactly what is expected of them. By breaking these lofty goals into specific tangible actions and creating meaning as well as a sense of purpose this is one of the most powerful ways to bridge the gap between strategy and successful execution.

BUILDING A WINNING BUSINESS STRATEGY

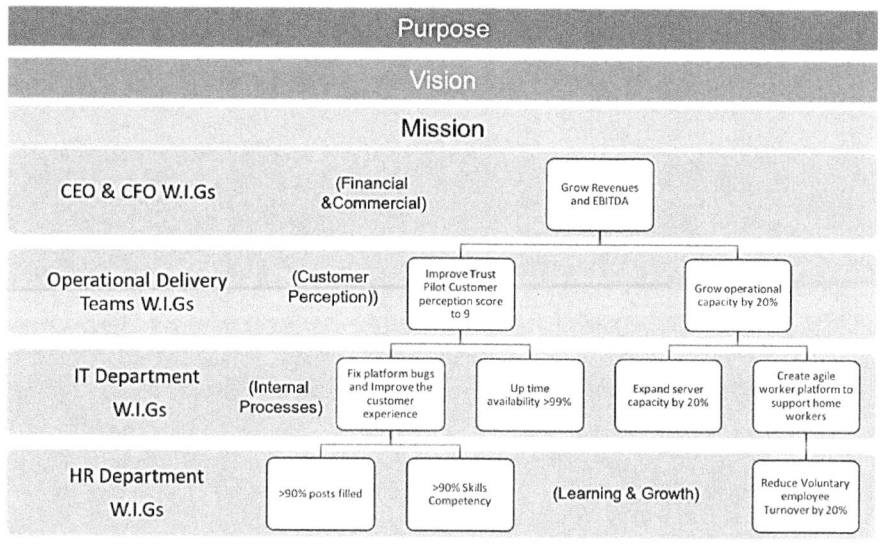

Figure 44 W.I.G ladder showing the departmental contributions to the overall purpose

They do say that the best way to eat an elephant is a bite at a time, so by breaking the sometimes lofty goals down into specific actions and showing how each of them contributes to the demise of the whole elephant is a fundamental part of the selling and delivering on the strategy. Having an organisation that is perfectly clear on the overall purpose but following the CEO's speech are left to interpret how this will be delivered is a recipe for potential disaster. The W.I.G ladder creates a line of sight from the very bottom to the very top of the organisation where everyone plays their very important part in the overall success. Without the W.I.G ladder and Strategy Map the various departments and teams do not always understand or appreciate the contribution that their colleagues are making and so you get departments that have overlapping or seemingly contradictory goals which causes confusion, conflict and people end up wasting too much time fighting internal battles and forget about the mission.

You could imagine that each department is a different team member on a football pitch where the departments all work together in a complimentary way to achieve succes. Just telling them all to win or alternatively not to loose could create confusion even though they know what the overall goals are, they are unsure of the part they play or how to achieve success.

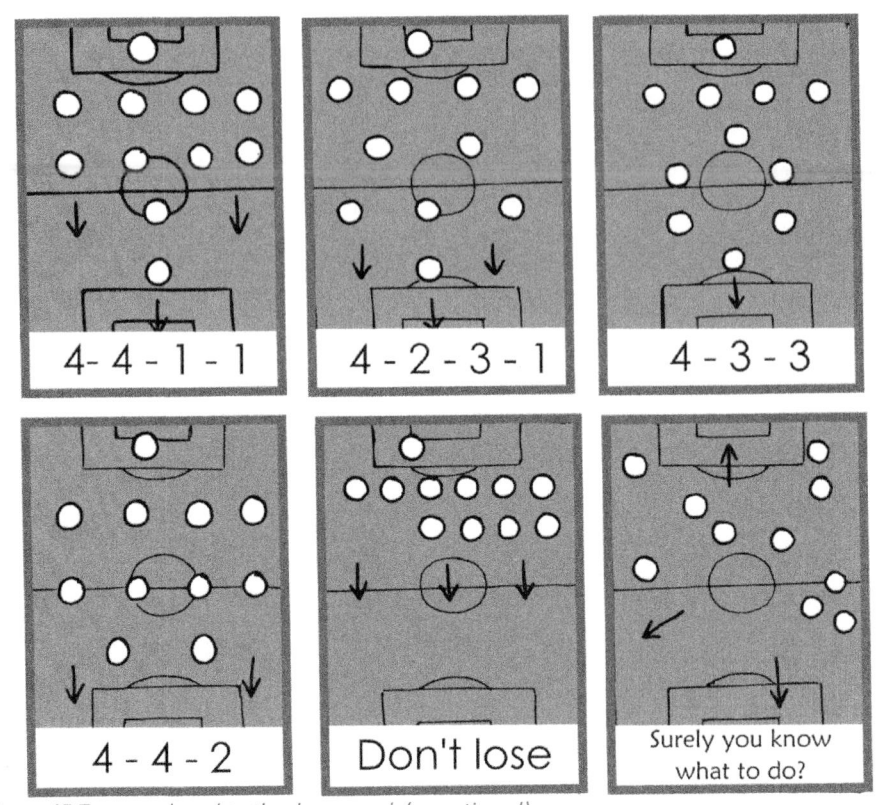

Figure 45 Teamwork makes the dreamwork (sometimes!)

Knowing what the collective end goal is does not provide a guarantee of success, you have to get the organisational design right and ensure that each department knows exactly what they are responsible for, what is expected of them and how their success contributes to the overall mission of the organisation. Once you have got your departments working together and aligned you then need to increase the magnification on the organisational microscope and look at what people are challenged with at the individual level.

PEOPLE PLAY FOR REAL WHEN YOU KEEP SCORE

We all know the difference between playing for fun and playing for real. When we are kicking a ball about on the park or throwing a few hoops on the basketball court, there inevitably comes a point during the preambles when someone says, "right lets pick sides and have a game". As you start keeping score, the intensity of the effort is increased and everyone gives more of themselves in a bid to win the game but equally important, people try harder as they do not want to let their teammates down. In team sports the goals are clear and the objective of scoring more points than the other team is well understood.

So after playing football at the weekend you return to Monday morning at the office. How do you know at any given moment if you are winning or losing? Do you know what good looks like and what is expected of everyone on your team to achieve it? I have had experiences with companies large and small that like to keep the score a secret from most of their employees. There are companies that are doing well but don't want their employees to start asking for more money, and companies that are not doing so well and seemingly start to rely on other less tangible indicators to assess how well they are doing.

I once asked a Director of a Plant Hire business what his measure of success was and he gave me a puzzled look. I reframed the question in more straightforward terms and asked "How do you know when you are doing well?", to which he replied "oh that's easy, there's a real buzz about the place". In another organisation that was losing money, I had introduced a balanced scorecard as part of the turnaround strategy and invited the senior team to a meeting where we could review the metrics and put plans in place to improve the situation. It was immediately obvious that key members of the senior team were shocked at the state of the company's finances and one of them remarked that he thought we were doing better than that because we all were so busy.

In the absence of clearly defined goals, with clear measures and accountability, the only real scoreboard that people have to go by is the clock. People start to measure performance by the amount of time they spend at the office. The whole culture drifts towards quantity of time rather than quality of outputs and performance. When managers ask that their people go the extra mile this is interpreted as putting in longer hours. In a company where nobody knows the score and how individuals are contributing, it then becomes almost impossible to recognise and reward good performance.

In organisations that have clearly defined goals, with aligned measures and KPI's that are visible and understood by all, the scoreboard overtakes the significance of the clock. Ensuring that the KPI's and the scores are used in a positive way to reward, encourage and incentivie will improve engagement and team goals and will unify the people to perform better.

Figure 46 Keeping score and playing for real!

"There are only three measurements that tell you nearly everything you need to know about your organisation's overall performance: employee engagement, customer satisfaction, and cash flow. It goes without saying that no company, small or large, can win over the long run without energized employees who believe in the mission and understand how to achieve it."

— Jack Welch

12 The Balanced Scorecard

"If you can't measure it, you can't improve it." – Peter Drucker

If you want to get better at something like playing golf, you would count how many shots it takes you to complete all 18 holes of the course and in between each game you would practice with purpose on improving your swing and how you read the course. Over a period of time your golf handicap would improve and you would not lose faith as you would be able to see the total number of shots trending downwards. Of course, like the stock market the trend line will have some volatility between each round but overall as you get better it should move in the right direction. Keeping with the golf analogy, you would also check progress at each hole rather than count the total number of shots at the end. You would want to know if you were at, below or above par for each of the holes to try and keep your overall number of shots to a mimmum. By keeping score, identifying trends and looking at ways to improve you will effectively fine tune your performance to maintain a steady improvement in line with your goals. If you look back at the last 12 rounds of golf that you had played on a particular course you may be able to identify a hole that seems to be your Achilles heel whereby on average you take an additional 5 shots on that hole over par. You resolve to practice that particular hole and experiment with club selection and approach to the green until you have mastered the hole and brought it back into par with the rest of your game.

Bringing this into the business context if you look at each of the months in the financial year you will have varying targets and expectations of where you need to be each month to achieve the overall performance depending on any seasonal variability as highlighted earlier. By breaking your year-end goals into weekly or monthly targets you will be able to monitor performance and allocate resources accordingly to ensure you keep on track. Dependent what industry you are in, what your strategy is and what your parameters for success are will determine the ways in which you keep score. Probably the most common form of measurement in business are the financial metrics around sales and profitability and other key performance indicators will generally be established that will act as pre-determinants of the right kind of financial results, here are a few examples:-

- **Hotel industry** – Room occupancy rates.
- **Construction rental industry** – Asset utilisation rates.
- **Automotive industry** – Vehicles sold.
- **Airline Industry** – Passenger occupancy rates.
- **Conveyancing** – Number of cases closed.
- **Law industry** – No of billed hours.
- **Media** – Advertising space sold.

As human beings we like to keep score and we generally perform better when we understand where we are now and where we need to be. Our competitive nature kicks in and why try and improve on the previous week or the previous month and we generally like to get regular feedback on how well we are doing. In this next section, I will share with you the experiences that I have had over the years with scorecards both good and bad and how to optimise the creation of your scorecard to get the very best performance. Here are a few simple rules to follow to create the perfect balanced scorecard:-

1. **Be clear about what you are trying to achieve** – This sounds fairly obvious but when choosing the appropriate measures for your scoreboard you should always ask – "will knowing this metric and acting upon it deliver our Wildly Important Goals".
2. **Get the team involved** – Involvement equals commitment and getting the team involved in creating their own scorecard will go a long way towards its successful implementation. By discussing the various measures and the goals you are trying to achieve, having team members think about and contribute with their own metrics is very valuable as this then creates team ownership for the scorecard which is far better than the manager creating the scorecard and asking them to fill in.
3. **Make sure the cost of measurement does not outweigh the value of knowing the measure** – this is closely related to rule number 1 but sometimes what seems like a perfectly reasonable thing to measure on a monthly basis is in fact devilishly difficult to obtain and requires so much manual intervention and interpretation that the cost of the measure outweighs its value.

A key pitfall to guard against is to make sure you do not create a cottage industry around the collection and measurement of data to the extent that you lose sight of what it is your are trying to achieve, which brings me nicely on to the next rule.

4. **Keep the number of measurements to a minimum** – this can be tested as the team discusses each of the measures and the reasons for including them on the scorecard. Is the measurement being captured at a high enough level. An example here would be if you wanted to measure the overall electricity consumption of a building, ideally you would have one measurement that does just that and not measurements from each of the sub meters on each of the eleven floors. A good way to think about this is to imagine the cockpit of a Boeing 747 airplane. There are literally hundreds of dials and switches but you would expect that the people that had designed the ergonomics of the cockpit had removed redundancy as much as possible to ensure they do not to overly distract the pilots. Business is very complicated just like flying a plane so even if you are trying to keep the measurements to a minimum you may end up with a full cockpit. I am no pilot but I would guess there are no lights in the cockpit that flash when they have run out of vegetarian meals. I am also pretty confident that there are some dials that are more important than others such as fuel, air speed, altitude and direction.

5. **Do not include measures just because you can** – this is a little bit like rule number four but sometimes I see teams wanting to include measures just because the data is easy to obtain or system generated. Just because your new system has an automatic warning to indicate the lack of vegetarian meals, this does not make it a candidate for taking up valuable real estate in the cockpit.

6. **Beware of unintended consequences** – the whole idea of introducing measurement and a scorecard is to get the results that you want. Be careful to fully think through how people might be tempted to behave as a result of the measures being introduced. A famous fast food restaurant introduced a measure for waste food at the end of each shift in an attempt to reduce waste. The unintended consequence of the metric changed the behaviour of the restaurant workers to such an extent that they started cooking to order in the last hour of the shift. This reduced the amount of waste but increased the average customer wait time to unacceptable levels.

7. **Use both lead and lag measures** – to get the results you desire. A simple example to explain what I mean by lead and lag measures is to think about loosing weight. A lag measure is when you get on the scales at the end of the week and measure how successful your

efforts have been. A suitable lead measure would be a daily measure of your calorie intake or number of visits to the gym. Many companies will use only lag or after the fact measures to run their business. They will produce a month end set of financials that will either be above or below expectations but until the finance team turns the handle at the end of the month the rest of the senior team sit there with their fingers crossed hoping that there will no nasty surprises. The monthly meetings then turn into a post mortem on what went wrong or the monthly snapshot will be used to confirm that they believe they are still heading in the right direction. Its analogy time again and we will use weight loss as an example, a lag measure is when you step once a week on the scales to see if you have lost weight. Some good lead measures to support this would be to go to the gym three times a week and consume less than 2500 calories a day. If you stick to your gym visits and daily calorie intake targets you are less likely to be surprised (apart from pleasantly) when you get on the scales at the end of the week. In your organisation you may have a goal of increasing sales through the acquisition of new customers and so a suitable lag measure would be the number of new customers added and a suitable lead measure would be number of new customer visits in the month. The lead measures are the inputs to get the desired outputs or lag results. If you only use lag measures in your business it will be like running your business by looking through the rear view mirror. Lead measures change behaviors that affect future results so it is best to have the right mix of lead and lag measures to give you the best possible understanding of where you are and where you are heading.

8. **Be clear with the team on what the scoreboard will be used for** – the introduction of a Balanced Scorecard can be met with skepticism and fear among your people. They may be concerned that the targets are deliberately set too high and this will be used as an individual performance improvement tool. Introducing a scoreboard is a key step in creating a culture of responsibility and accountability and so this must be handled sensitively but if it is done in the right way it can be a positive experience all round. In my experience once people's concerns are put at ease and the scoreboard has been running for a few months, as long as you and the senior team react to the results in a positive and reinforcing way then the scoreboard will become a positive motivator for the entire business. The introduction of the scorecard does however mean that things are going to change, unfortunately in business when

management say change, people hear loss. The balanced scorecard is ultimately all about improving business perfromance and therefore improving the overall job security and development prospects for all concerned.

9. **Accept a period of calibration** – once you have built your scoreboard and agreed the targets for each measure including when and where the data will come from it is then best to agree a period of calibration to test the scoreboard in practice over a number of months. It would be very difficult to build a scoreboard from scratch and launch it without the need for further modification or calibration and accepting this as a team from the outset will reduce the pressure on the team to get all the measures right on day one and will give them valuable experience of working with the scoreboard before it gets locked down and standardised. In the calibration phase you need to check and validate the data that is being collected from the business, make sure that it does not violate rule 3 and become too expensive to collect relative to its value, make sure you have the target sets right, make sure that you are interpreting the scorecard correctly and you are clear what the corrective actions would need to be for a given set of results. Are the measures giving you what you want or do you need to change the measurement parameters to get the results that you are looking for.

10. **Set Goldilocks targets** – the targets set need to be just right, not too hot and not too cold. If all you are doing is having a scoreboard full of green lights every month then this will present too little challenge to the team. Conversely looking at a scoreboard that is full of red lights every month could make the team lose confidence and give up. The targets need to be challenging but achievable and the target parameters for red and green lights should be adjusted accordingly through the calibration stage and then reviewed regularly to keep them in the Goldilocks zone as your performance improves.

11. **Beware the dreaded amber** – I always try to avoid having an amber zone on the scorecard. Amber stands for **amber - guity** and if you are looking at a scorecard full of amber lights on your scorecard you do not know if you are nearly winning or nearly loosing. Having only red and green lights makes the reporting and commentary on the scorecard much more efficient. It's a little bit like reporting triage where you can focus your attention purely on the red lights, this makes the review meetings much more productive as you get to spend your valuable management time where it is needed most.

12. **Make sure you are on trend, that is all that matters** – having cautioned about making sure that you do not set the targets too high there are ways in which you can keep the team motivated by showing the performance trend on the scorecard.

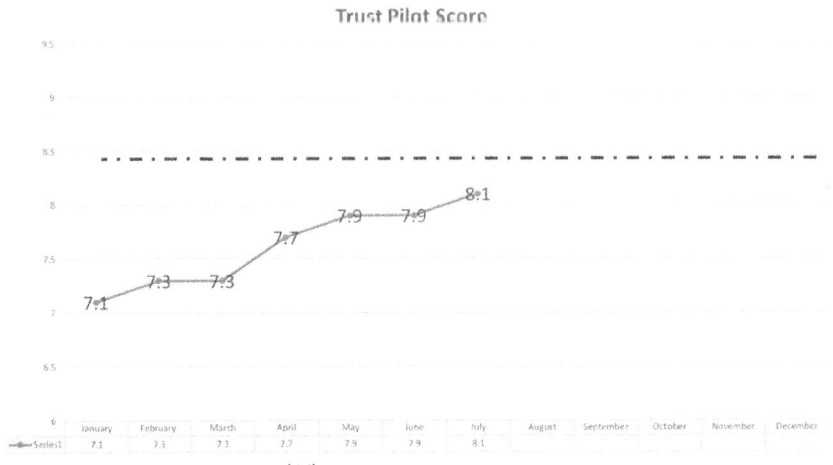

Trust Pilot Score

	January	February	March	April	May	June	July	August	September	October	November	December
Series1	7.1	7.3	7.3	7.7	7.9	7.9	8.1					

Figure 47 Customer perception trend V's target

In the above example, even though the scorecard would have had a red light in every month of the year from January to July, showing a positive trend that clearly shows that that target can be achieved at the current rate of improvement can be a real motivator. This plays to the principles of rule 8 where you have an opportunity as a senior team to reward the efforts of the team as they are clearly moving in the right direction. One particularly poor example of the use of the scorecard was from a CEO that I used to work for where he would say that "red blobs cost jobs". This little heuristic had a negative effect on the team that encouraged artistic license on the gathering and the interpretation of the data and unsurprisingly the red blobs miraculously disappeared. Red lights should be looked at as opportunities for improvement where each team is challenged to think of creative and innovative ways to improve the performance of the business. Green lights should also be a cause for celebration large and small.

KEEPING THE BALANCE IN THE SCORECARD

The creation of the scorecard to provide balance will go a long way towards delivering the long term success. Balance in business is a little bit like balance in life and too much of any one thing can potentially be unhealthy for you over the longer term. When Jim Collins was looking at what he calls 10x companies for his study on organisations that had outperformed their competitors by a factor of 10, he found that balance was achieved between the long and short term goals of the business but their core ideologies also provided the right balance for day to day decisions. At 3M where employees were directed to spend 15% of their time working on pet projects which is a policy that obviously balances the short term demands of the here and now with future innovation. Many of the companies used in the study by Jim Collins were founded with a vision and a core ideology that would be more than just about making money, these businesses were forever mindful not to sacrifice their longer term objectives for short term financial goals. When the Ford Motor Company ran into difficulties in the 1980's its management team held a strategic review that went to the heart of what the company and founder Henry Ford stood for, which was in stark contrast to the firefighting approach adopted by its industry rival General Motors.

The companies that survive and thrive over the longer term make regular decisions that keep them in balance by refusing to abide by the tyranny of the OR, where companies have to choose between staying true to their core ideology and stimulating progress in the short term. What Jim Collins refers to as the genius of the AND such as making a profit and investing heavily in employee development. These companies balance their core ideologies with the relentless pursuit of continuous improvement of their products and services.

Finance Director – "what if we invest all this money in developing our employees and they leave!"
Human Resources Director – "what happens if we don't and they stay".

LONG TERM MEASUREMENTS

As well as keeping score of metrics on the scoreboard that you want your teams to influence on a weekly or monthly basis there are also some measurements that can be taken over a longer time period that will give you a greater sense of where your business is perfoming from a cultural perspective. Looking at employee engagement surveys and the depth and quality of the performance development reviews can be a good way to check you are on course but these are metrics that you can capture just once or twice a year. They are still worth including on the scorecard as your strategic transformation will be measured in years. When creating your balanced scorecard it is useful to think of putting the right measures and incentives in place to get your business running like clockwork. If you were to remove the back from an old mechanical clock you would see cogs of various shapes and sizes. Some of the cogs will be spinning incredibly fast some will be running a little slower and there will be some cogs that are running so slow that you cannot see them actually moving with the naked eye. This is analogous to having measures and feedback on an hourly, daily, weekly, monthly, six monthly and annual basis and the constant monitoring and calibration of the short feedback measures will ensure the annual metrics are in the right direction. Reacting in the right way to weekly lag measures will effectively generate lead actions to affect the monthly and annual measures.

CARROT AND STICK MOTIVATION

Dependent on your leadership style you may have a preference for how you like to motivate people but studies have found that motivational factors are context specific and sometimes the best way to motivate is the carrot and at other times it's the stick. If you refer back to the section on sales where I produced a notional incentive plan for a salesperson where they could earn a 120% performance bonus but then this bonus was reduced if other sales parameters were not met. This was done to get the maximum benefit from the salesperson by tapping into the psyche of the sales person based on scientific psychological principles.

People are more motivated by what the stand to lose than what they stand to gain and they hate losing more than they like winning. The stick punishment approach in business can be very cost effective and it works better for the same cost. For example a £100 fine for not achieving a particular outcome would be much more effective at driving team behaviour than a £100 reward for achieving it.

When considering ways in which to capture, report and incentivise against your balanced scorecard you need to consider the best way to present the metrics to achieve the greatest result. To make the introduction of the scorecard successful, you need to turn the business into a game that all the participants want to play, that is both fair and transparent and that will engage and motivate everyone. Fining people £100 for not achieving a particular result could have them running for the hills but if at the beginning of the year you put a £12,000 team pot of money up as a bonus and then introduced a fair and transparent fine system against it, this would more likely achieve better results than rewarding the team £100 each time you get the desired behaviour and showing the bonus pot building up to a potential £12,000. Both schemes would have the same commercial parameters but the first would be far more persuasive, starting the year with a £12,000 pot of money for the team would make them more determined to keep hold of it. Another powerful way to motivate is to go for more frequent small rewards than larger ones over the longer term. As human beings we favour short term gratification over longer term gains. How many people do you know that want to lose weight that will frequently binge on junk food. The bottom line is that we are all addicted to now and presenting a team with the prospect of a £12,000 annual bonus is not as powerful as presenting the team with a £1,000 monthly bonus. Once again the commercial parameters of the incentive are the same but the regular rewards are likely to be much more effective than a larger reward placed at the end of the year.

The way in which you chose to introduce your scorecard will depend very much on your culture and your industry, it is about being sensitive to your people and understanding what would be the best way to get everybody engaged. The financial incentive examples for instance would work very well in a call centre sales environment and significantly less well in a not for profit charity where the chances are the employees or volunteers would be seeking different forms of achievement and fulfillment from their work.

During the introduction of the scorecard, if you are minded to link financial incentives and/or disincentives to the results, again this is something that you could do by consultation with the employeesto ensure you get the result you are looking for.

What you will find however following the introdcution of the scorecard, that your teams will be much more engaged and interested in the performance of the business, the Gamification (healthy competition) of the achievement of business results will improve your teams knowledge and understanding of the key metrics and performance areas.

"You cannot hit a target you cannot see and you cannot see a target you do not have"
– Zig Ziglar

There are some pitfalls that you need to be mindful of if you are thinking of introducing some financial incentives against the metrics in your scorecard. If you create your scorecard using KPI's and targets that are achieveable but challenging and then introduce financial incentives for the achievement of a particular score, once the score is reached, the correct thing to do is raise the bar to drive continous improvement. Once incentives are paid against certain KPI's any attempt to re-calibrate the target upwards will be met by resistance from the benefactors of the incentive scheme. Several years ago I introduced an incentive scheme in the business to reduce aged debt to a certain level by the year end. Sure enough by the end of the year we had managed to reduce aged debt from over £4M to just over £700K. Everyone got paid as the target had been achieved but then in the subsequent months the aged debt started to rise again. When we tried to tackle the issue of the raising debt this time around the team were more concerned with what the incentive scheme would look like. The introduction of incentives against metrics can be very successful in achieving one off spectacular results but it's a little bit like squeezing the toothpaste out of the tube it becomes impossible to put it back in.

13 Holding each other to account

In the years I've been thinking and talking about leadership, I've come to realise that the desperate need for accountable leaders is the fundamental challenge organisations are facing today. Vince Molinaro

Having created the strategy and pulled together the wildly important goals (W.I.G's), then having broken these goals down into specific actions and disseminated them across the workforce together with a compelling reward scoreboard the final part of the delivery process is about accountability. If you do not get this part right there is still every chance that your strategy and change programme will fail. What follows is a short scenario that unfortunately plays itself out in boardrooms up and down the country.
At the start of the meeting we go through the actions from the minutes of the previous meeting, the chair calls out to each of the participants in turn for an update and all without exception will say that there action is ongoing or is in hand. Some of the actions are now a couple of months overdue but everyone in the meeting knows just how busy they have all been. The meeting members do not give each other a hard time because essentially they are all in the same boat and deadlines are passed without consequence and accountability becomes none existent. As the meeting progresses

throughout the day, the meeting members contribute to the discussion and agree to take away even more actions in the knowledge that failing to deliver on the actions will not be frowned upon, but at least if they take the actions it will be stalled with them until they can find the time to do it rather than it go to someone else.

This particular scenario maybe an extreme example as the meeting participants probably take on the actions with the best intentions but as there are no apparent consequences for missing deadlines on these meeting actions, the closing out of the actions will always come second to the day to day urgent requirements of their position. I have gone into businesses and as part of my discovery phase I have asked for copies of the previous 12 months meeting minutes so that I can get up to speed on some of the key issues. What I have found in some cases are that actions have been ongoing for months and months and you get a distinct feeling that very senior managers have been coming together for a full day meeting every month and essentially end up talking about the same things with no break from the vicious cycle. The language of the senior team then becomes defensive, what should be a monthly meeting to drive the business forward turns into a collective "pity party", where they all turn up to complain about the customers, the competition, the state of the economy and how busy they are. This learned helplessness can make for a very depressing monthly meeting with only the comfort food on the buffet at lunchtime giving any sense of relief. If this sounds like your company and I sincerely hope for your sake that it is not, then do not worry too much as help is at hand. It is never too late to draw a line in the sand and bring back accountability.

Firstly it is all about recogising how busy everyone is but gaining agreement and buyin that you will always as a team be very busy and unless the team start to actively plan their Quadrant 2 activities and stick to them, then you will never be able to take the business forward. You need to draw a line in the sand and the chair needs to declare that when actions are accepted in meetings and completion dates are agreed that the actions do indeed get done. Holding each other to account is a function of the board or the senior leadership team in any organisation and a healthy team fit for the long term will do just that. The disciplined execution of a business strategy requires that the discipline of accountability and responsibility is clearly understood and that the chair of the meetings creates an expectation that things will get done.

Being part of the senior leadership team of an organisation for you as an individual means that your performance will be judged on the overall performance of the business and you have a obligation to speak up and challenge appropriately, anything that you feel needs to be given closer scrutiny. I always say that good leadership is wanting to hear, what you do not necersarily want to hear. There are countless lessons from history ranging from the Challenger shuttle disaster to the Iraq weapons of mass destruction and the global banking crisis where seamingly hundreds if not thousands of people towed the party line, did not rock the boat and collectively suffered from cognative tunnel blindness, only to subsequently became experts after the fact. I refer you back to the quotation at the begining of this section and our need for accountable leaders with the courage and conviction to hold themselves and their teams to account.

14 Bringing it all together

We shall not cease from exploration, and the end of all our exploring will be to arrive where we started and know the place for the first time.

T. S. Eliot

Its been quite a journey but I hope by now you think it has been a worthwhile one. We started looking at demystifying the dark art of strategy on the understanding that through the book I would give you a practical guide to strategy formulation and a systematic process for working through the various phases culminating in the execution to achieve the winning results. We initially spent a lot of time in the discovery phase understanding what your business is good at and what it wants to be famous for, we looked at the competition and the market and made choices on how and where your business would fit and flourish. We looked at things that could be reduced and eliminated as well as raised and created to strengthen your offering and free up sufficient resources. In the chapter on people we spent time understanding the benefits of how to create an engaged workforce and went through the full employee lifecycle and talent management planning, as this is fundamentally important for the delivery of long term strategy. In the chapter on sales we looked into historical sales and analysed ways in which the recent past is a good indicator of where to start with your sales strategy going forward. We looked at the size and types of customer accounts along with the attractiveness, maturity and life cycle of your chosen markets so you could make the right choices on where best to focus your sales efforts. We looked at the best ways to incentivise your sales team to get the results that you want as well as developing an understanding about the correct way to set order intake targets along with an appreciation of the sales composition and seasonal timings to deliver sustainable success going forward. We then looked at the various strategic choices whether they be cost leadership or product/service focus and built a buisness plan with scenario modelling to take acount of risks and opportunities which would then continue to be modelled and controlled throughout the delivery of the strategy to make the necsessary course adjustments.

When the strategic design process was complete, we turned our attention to how the strategy would be sold to your two most important audiences, your employees and your customers. We constructed a brand ladder and a strategy map that worked through the logical sequence of getting the right people, working on the very best systems and processes, delivering value to the client and resulting in superior financial and commercial performance. As well as creating a compelling vision and a burning platform for change we explored the difficulties of how to overcome resistance and inertia from the company's culture and that this was essential if your change initiative was to survive and thrive. To beat the odds and ensure your strategy does not become one of the 70% failure rate statistics, we then looked at the disciplined execution of the strategy by focusing on the Wildly Important, breaking the lofty goals into specific actions, creating a compelling scoreboard and then finished off by driving home the importance of holding one another to account.

To conclude this final section, I would like to thank for sticking with it, and hopefully you have found the content both practical and useful. There are no guarantees I can offer in summary apart from saying that your chances of success in your strategy will have been greatly improved as a result of following these tried and tested methods and processes. Business and strategy are not difficult but they are complicated and its not about following a set recipe for succes but being equipped with enough knowledge and tools to deal with a range of circumstances that you may face in your professional life as a leader. I wish you every success for the future.　　Good luck.

ABOUT THE AUTHOR

Steve Farmer started out as an Engineering Apprentice Electrician who later tooks roles in commercial and operational management. Over the last 15 years Steve has held a number of senior leadership roles at CEO, COO & MD level, predomenantly in the UK Construction, Engineering and Rail sectors. Along with his studies in Engineering and an MBA he has read hundreds of books on business strategy, leadership, negotiating skills and persuasion. His career in the UK has has not been immune from significant disruption and recessionary times, all have contributed to a broad business perspective gained across all levels of the organisation. Steve is an optimist and an innovator and believes that the best way to get results is through the engagement and motivation of his teams to achieve outstanding results. In this his first book Steve brings together and shares valuable insight into creating a winning business strategy.

BIBLIOGRAPHY

First Things First, Prentice Hall & IBD; Reprint edition (1 Jun. 1995), *Stephen R. Covey (Author)*
The 7 Habits of Highly Effective People, Simon and Schuster; Reprinted Edition edition (4 Jan. 2004), *Stephen R. Covey (Author)*
4 Disciplines of Execution: Getting Strategy Done, Simon & Schuster UK; UK ed. edition (21 July 2015) *Sean Covey (Author*
The Fifth Discipline: The art and practice of the learning organization: Second edition, Random House Business; 2Rev Ed edition (6 April 2006), Peter Senge
Built To Last: Successful Habits of Visionary Companies, Random House Business; New Ed edition (1 Sept. 2005), Jim Collins
Made to Stick: Why Some ideas Survive and Others Die, Randon h (2007), Chip and Heath, Dan Heath (Author)
Rich Dad Poor Dad: What the Rich Teach Their Kids About Money That the Poor and Middle Class Do Not!, Plata Publishing; Second edition (27 April 2017), Robert T. Kiyosaki (Author)
Brain Rules (Updated and Expanded): 12 Principles for Surviving and Thriving at Work, Home, and School, Pear Press; Second edition (8 May 2014), John Medina (Author)
21st Century Leadership, 21CPL Productions 2010, Dave Stitt & Paul Fox (Authors)
Deal, T.E. and Kennedy, A.A. (1982) Corporate Cultures: The Rites and Rituals of Corporate Life. Addison Wesley Publishing Company, Reading, 126.
On the origin of shared beliefs (and corporate culture) First published: 08 November 2010 Eric Van den Steen
Organizational Culture and Leadership, Edgar H. Schein. 1992. Jossey-Bass Publishers, San Francisco, CA. 418 pages. ISBN: 1-55542-487-2.

Printed in Great Britain
by Amazon